SELF

EMPOWERMENT

SELF EMPOWERMENT

RECLAIM YOUR PERSONAL POWER

REVITALIZE YOUR COMMUNITY,
YOUR COUNTRY AND THE WORLD

Chrystol Clark Harris

Don R. Harris

CARMEL HIGHLANDS PUBLISHING

Carmel, California

This book is sold with the understanding that the subject matter covered herein is of a general nature and does not constitute medical, legal or other professional advice for any specific individual or situation.

Printed in the United States of America
1   2   3   4   5   6   7   8   9   0

Library of Congress Cataloging in Publication Data

Harris, Chrystol Clark.
　　Self-empowerment: reclaim your personal power: revitalize your community, your country and the world / Chrystol Clark Harris, Don R. Harris.
　　p. cm.
　　Includes bibliographical references.
　　Preassigned LCCN: 93-070811.
　　ISBN 1-883134-38-2

　　1. Self-actualization (Psychology). 2. Self-realization. 3. Change (Psychology) 4. Social change. 5. New age movements. I. Harris, Don R II. Title.

BF637.S4H37 1993　　　　　　　158'. 1
　　　　　　　　　　　　　　　　　　QBI93-20684

This book was produced and designed by
　　Ex Libris Publishing Services, Los Gatos, California

Cover design by Bunne Hartmann,
　　Hartmann Design Studios, Carmel , California

PUBLISHING
P. O. Box 22664
Carmel, California 93922

To my son Trevor Lucas,
my greatest teacher and healer.
With love and gratitude,
                    —*Chrystol*

To my sons Michael and Dale ,
who have taught me so much.
With love and appreciation,
                    —*Don*

CONTENTS

Chapter 7—A Vision of the World We Want   141

ACKNOWLEDGMENTS

To Matthew, my guardian angel and spiritual guide.

My deepest appreciation and love to my husband, and life partner. His sense of wonder, adventure and eternal optimism has been a source of inspiration and delight. Holding each other's hand through the writing of this book has given a new meaning to the words - sharing, trust and intimacy.

My thanks and gratitude to my dear friends who generously share their love, humor, joy, understanding, wisdom and support. Their spirituality, courage, enlightenment and humanity have been a source of inspiration as our lives, souls and hearts touch.

Nancy Sturgis, Bob Hoover, Juli King, Jane Feaver, Maureen Robertson, John Clark, Michael Lavelle, Patrick and Roy Connolly, Susan Emerson, Laurie McCullem, Miriam and Earl Selby, Betsy Brown, Agatha Nagy, Tara, Don Kennedy, Dennis Evans, M.D., Don Hovland, Marg and Don Mogridge, Joe Brawley, Diane and Don Critchley, Marlene and Gene Wakaruk, Christine Sturgis, Erin and Charles Ganzon, Father Charlie Moore, Kris Swanson. Thank you to all those I did not name, I carry you in my heart as well.

Special thanks and love to my sisters and brother, Darlene Ousman and Debbie and Earl Ditchfield, although we were not raised together, the bond is there.

With love to my father, Clifford Reid Ditchfield, my mother, Lila Rosalie Markey and my stepfather, Mark Markey, you are with me in spirit.

Don and Eileen Wilbur and Iline and Lloyd Moffat, relatives who are also my friends, thanks for being there.

CCH

My families, both close and extended have had great influence and deserve a special kind of recognition. To my Mom and Dad, Jack & Gladys Harris; to my sisters, Jacqueline Merritt and Shirley Ramstedt and their kids; to my close cousins, Adele and Worth Keene and their family who made me part of their family. With my parents married 52 years, lots of travel together and large family get together's, we had a special kind of bond and community. We didn't choose each other overtly, but we enjoyed, and appreciated each other and stuck together through conflict as well as joy because we didn't know any other options, sharing many experiences of growth and fun.

To my many friends along the way, too many to mention but in particular Ron Chandler and Herman Miller.

More recently, I want to thank the people who were instrumental in causing me to change my life more positively, change my job, my work, my living location and my life, Gary Heald, and Bill Dozier. There are still changes, new experiences and new people. The men who have been close to me, individually and in men's groups have influenced me greatly. I also wish to recognize the people I met and with whom I have become close while living eight months at Esalen Institute, and Esalen Institute itself, its identity, personality and programs which have been very meaningful on my current path.

My last and most important thanks goes to a woman I met over two years ago. We saw and experienced each other's spirits, hopes, hurts, frailties and strengths and have traveled around the world and through many experiences together. We have worked, suggested, criticized and experienced this book being born with the hope it can help people individually, our country and the world as writing it has helped us. She is now my wife and our path continues with passion for life, hoping to serve and help make things better.

DRH

Thanks go to Colin Ingram, who we came to as first-time writers with a rough document and high hopes. He criticized and praised our work, advised and contributed to our writing.

Special thanks and appreciation to Dove Grace with her insight and feeling for this book, we appreciate her help, her contributions, her understanding of what we are trying to accomplish. She could read between the lines, the meaning we were trying to convey. She contributed substantially through her dedication, editing and proofing. She also became our friend.

To Juli King of Merrill West Publishing, our publishing guardian angel and special friend. She encouraged us, taught us and answered the many questions along the way. To Robert Erdmann for his generous time in his seminar and his personal inspiration and example. Great thanks to Julie Kranhold and Bunne Hartmann, our book designers, for their creative forces. They both put in wonderful special effort when it was needed. To many others who have helped and educated us in this process.

Our final hope and thanks is for you the reader. We haven't said it all, but rather what we could in the space of these pages and with the ideas that have come to us. There are many solutions we can draw upon and implement. Each reader may have ideas of his or her own and even where they differ they don't need to conflict, they can all support each other in making the world a better place. Share your ideas and your own hopes and passions. This is a book of hope and optimism because we know you and we can make a difference. Enjoy, experience your power and have a better life.

SELF

EMPOWERMENT

INTRODUCTION

*T*he purpose of this book is to not only show how we have given away our personal power but more importantly, how each of us can get our power back. Also we address how our power can be used to effect positive change around us, in our country and in the world.

We begin to regain our personal power by looking within ourselves, at our own values and beliefs: How do we live up to our own highest standards of integrity? What is right for us? What is our purpose in life? How can we become exponents of our spiritual values? What is the meaning of community? What kind of world do we want? Living by our highest inner standard is the best if not the only way to live.

No one is totally disempowered. Being empowered consistently and at higher levels can bring joy, happiness and appreciation to our lives. An entire new quality and effectiveness will become a permanent way of living. We are not only bodies and minds but more importantly spiritual beings. By experiencing all of these working in unison and in integrity we can have a richness in experience that we had not before thought possible. Problems and questions take on a different meaning from our enhanced and new perspective. By making even small changes in our lives we will gradually rise to new heights of empowerment.

Our writing isn't the beginning of this movement, but hopefully a guide and an inspiration for people struggling to be empowered and to make a difference in the world and who are no longer willing to be impotent victims.

Many of us have become angry because of the problems we see in our country and in the world. Worse than this current anger is maybe a more deep seated anger that we allowed this to happen. This reflects on us more in that a current problem can be passed off as just a mistake. A long term problem on the other hand, makes us look at our approach, our values and our effectiveness and also the greater task of bringing things back in line from further afield.

There exists a tremendous groundswell of unchanneled dissatisfaction, fear and frustration that is beginning to turn to anger and, as the urban riots show, sometimes to rage. How shall we begin to address these issues that seem so overwhelming and intractable? Should our first steps be toward becoming citizen-activists, revolutionaries, who by our individual and collective wills are able to force change? If so, it is important to first focus on improving our individual selves before trying to change the world. Many of our leading thinkers today believe that we must start with ourselves, that the conditions in the world are a reflection of conditions within each of us, and the world won't change until we first change ourselves. Because of these trends in thought, all sorts of personal development teachings have flourished in America.

What does this portend for our country? Can personal growth complement effective service to society? In India there are "enlightened" people called masts. They are called masts because they stand perfectly upright and still, rarely moving, so that they resemble the mast of a boat. Begging bowls are attached around their necks, and respectful worshippers, sensing their holiness, feed, clean and otherwise care for them. This is spiritual renunciation in the extreme. These masts may well be in communion with God, and this is not to deny their place or the path they have chosen. But they do not interact with the physical world.

For most of us, withdrawing from the world is not our goal. We live in a world economy and world environment whether we want to or not. We Americans are dynamic and progressive. We are, at heart, shakers and movers. We want to help shape our nation and our destiny, not sit back and have it done for us by others. The thrust of this book is that we individually, have too long been disengaged from our country and the world around us. We need to bring our intelligence, creativity and personal energy to bear upon its problems. At this time on our planet, our search for personal development and personal empowerment must coincide with social action.

There are opportunities for each of us. These opportunities present change all around us but where do we start? One of the ways we start is to get in touch with our inner-most selves. . . to suggest ways in which we can increase our available energy. Then we must identify our national problems, and focus our increasing energy on the most effective solutions to these problems. We believe that each of us can use our frustration and anger and apply it to begetting solutions and results. We can use our energy productively to save the nation-patient. We have the power to heal our wounds, and pump truth, integrity and common sense back into the life blood of our country.

We believe the search for happiness and fulfillment depends upon our looking deep within ourselves. We seek out our finest motives and ideals, and then we manifest these high ideals in the world around us. It is our intent through this book to create a positive feedback system. The more we find the best within ourselves, the more we can apply it to our world. And the more we do to help our world, the more we will be strengthened within. In our search for happiness and fulfillment, it is not time for us to be masts—it is time for us to be activists.

1

SELF-EMPOWERMENT, YOU, ME AND WE

WHAT IS SELF-EMPOWERMENT?

Self-empowerment is a belief system. It's a feeling that things are right within ourselves. It's a belief there is hope, a belief in ourselves, what we are and who we are. When we are feeling our power, we believe we can accomplish whatever has meaning for us and that the future is bright. Being self-empowered has a positive impact on all parts of our lives, from our health to our relationships. Even our ability to use what we know and how we feel about what we can do is affected. We have a core within us that knows what is right for us. We feel in balance, in harmony and in integrity.

Freedom from an ache in our gut or from fear of losing our job is self-empowerment. When we are feeling dissatisfaction or frustration we know how to get out of it. We no longer feel helpless, hopeless or trapped. Fear loses its death grip. It has been said that freedom from fear is more important than freedom from want.

When we feel our power, numbing out to get by or to avoid facing life is no longer the best solution. We can know what is right for us and find ways to live accordingly. We enjoy freedom, freedom to experience life to its fullest. We develop the capacity to feel our feelings without fear or shame, and become able to express them to others openly and to appreciate other's feelings as well. We can be open, not defended, because we don't have to fear.

The result of self-empowerment is the ability to recognize, restore, and live our lives with fun, joy, peace, harmony and purpose with ourselves and others; to find and do that which has deeper meaning for us; to act with conscious, life-advancing, constructive purpose; to identify and change that which impedes any of the above. The power to live this way is self-empowerment, experiencing the spiritual power within us.

BEING DISEMPOWERED IS NO FUN!

We were born with a zest for life. We wanted to learn. We wanted to enjoy. We wanted to be a part of—. Then we were probably shamed by someone or made to think we were bad, stupid or incapable. At a young age we were very dependent so we believed whatever was told to us.

Don: I grew up a dumb little kid, never with the right answers in school, always a little slow, always with a threat of being put back a grade. But, boy could I dream. I had vivid pictures of all sorts of exciting things, in color and with all the detail. The more people criticized (directly and indirectly) the more I liked my fantasy world. I could draw planes, scenery and all sorts of fun places to play and be. I even liked to make inventions.

The constant reminder that I wasn't learning as I was supposed to and that there was probably something wrong with me affected me in ways that I didn't understand until well into my adulthood. I couldn't share my dreams or creations because I should have been studying instead of drawing.

The phrase "having your spirit broken" is more than a casual expression. People talk about breaking horses or an animal's spirit to get them to obey. The process we want to discuss is mending our broken spirit and then nurturing and helping it to grow from the time it was wounded or stifled. This is empowerment. This is what we believe starts getting our power back.

Therapists who work with people involved with drugs or alcohol believe most of them quit maturing from the time they start into addictions. This also has been seen in cases of other traumas, such as mental, physical and sexual child abuse. If they are to mature and grow mentally and emotionally they have to start again from where they quit the maturing process.

Chrystol: When I was a year-and-a-half old, my father won custody of me. He had already divorced my mother. I remember him saying when I was about five, "I have a business, and don't have the time to raise a daughter". So for many years I was shuffled back and forth between his relatives, five brothers, a sister and several cousins. I never knew how long my stay would be. When I'd see my packed suitcase at the door, I knew I would be moving.

I would try to figure out what I must have done wrong. As time passed I began to feel there was something wrong with me and that's why no one wanted me around. After all, other kids lived in the same house all the time with their mom and dad or at least one parent. How come I didn't? Because I moved so much, each Christmas I worried that Santa wouldn't know where to bring my presents. I tried so hard to be a very good little girl so I would be loved, but I was never good enough. I hid my shame at not being wanted. I pushed my broken heart and my spirit so far inside me, I thought no one would ever be able to hurt or reject me again. Of course that really didn't work. As I grew up I became a

consummate actress and appeared well adjusted, well man-
nered and tried desperately to please everyone in my life. I
wanted to belong in a world where I never believed I fit or was
welcome. I also believed that love was earned, it was a form of
reward.

Eventually, I went to live with my alcoholic father and his 90-
year-old mother. He expected her to care for a 7-year-old when
she was too senile to take care of herself. He did remarry. It was
a marriage made in hell. It was a combat zone where I at times
feared for my life, having to step between two raging adults
before one of them got killed. His wife was as cruel emotionally
to me as he was physically. They were both emotional, sick and
out of control. I finally escaped this bedlam after I graduated from
high school at seventeen.

As many of us have had our spirits squelched or
broken, now we are afraid and don't know how to listen
to our inner selves. We can be so blocked we've lost the
knowledge that we have this spirit within us.

What are we talking about? As children we had an
insatiable curiosity and desire to learn and have fun. We
could play and be entertained by almost anything around
us. Our world was a joy, except when we were wet, hungry
or scolded.

Our spirit didn't use linear thinking, it just was and
it worked. It loved to learn, explore, loved people, life,
dogs, cats, flowers, mud and anything we could stick in
our mouths.

OUR POWER

*Our power comes from knowing and
tapping into our spirit.*

Defining our spirit, our inner non-linear thinking, is like defining love or electricity. We know some of the traits but a complete definition eludes us. From our experience the more we work with it, listen and try to understand it the more we realize its infiniteness. This vastness of spirit continues to the level stated in the Bible and most major religions claim that our spirit is joined in some way with a universal spirit and that there is a oneness or commonality between all of us. Some describe this as the God within us. We will use different terms for this which are very similar but have slightly different meanings throughout the book. Mostly we refer to the sense we are feeling at the time as our "inner guide." and sometimes as our centeredness, our conscience or our heart. We use conscience very little in this discussion as it has taken on a value or judgment meaning of right or wrong that may reflect others' opinions more than our spiritual feelings.

In addition to our body and mind we have a spiritual self. We have and need self-love, self-care, self-esteem, self-respect, self-honesty, self-acceptance, self-approval, self-empowerment and even selfishness. More about these later. In the past we were taught to love God first, others second and ourselves last. If it wasn't in this order, we were considered selfish and self-centered. Current views suggest the opposite. Being selfish to the extent we take care of ourselves and have rational self-interest and high self-esteem isn't wrong. We must love ourselves first and only then are we capable of loving others and in so doing we are showing our love for God. On the surface there appears to be a contradiction or paradox. However we don't believe there is. When we love ourselves, our beings, our spirit, we are not only loving us but God within us and our connectedness with others and all of creativity.

Our consciousness or wholeness will vary and become greater as we develop the capacity to explore our spiritual aspect more. We may experience this through just our own being, as feeling part of overall man's consciousness, or even a oneness with nature. Many things we experience are sensed at this level. There aren't enough words to describe a flower to someone who has never seen one before, let alone a sunset or beautiful seashore or landscape. Yet we can picture or visualize these things.

The sad part is many of us have lost touch with this innate child-spirit who embraces learning, but has been disempowered by all sorts of actions throughout our lives. The good news is we can get our power back. Our natural state is to be empowered and know our spiritual essence. If we open up again to this vast and wonderful natural resource within us we can more naturally progress on our spiritual and life path.

What does this mean? We can have a better, more meaningful life. We will no longer be victims. We will not need drugs or be "other" dependent. We can direct, live and enjoy our lives. We will become more aware of our desires and what is right for us versus what other people are telling us is right. Our work will be more meaningful and enjoyable. Our play will be more fun. We can re-experience the spontaneity of our youth. We can have wonderful healthy relationships, knowing where we begin and end (our boundaries) and where others begin and end and when we are joined together in oneness. Parents feel this oneness with their kids, lovers feel it with each other and we can all feel it with friends and communities. We talk about this with our teams, our gangs, our friends, our companies and our country. "That's the spirit" or we have spirit, a combined spirit!

BODY, MIND AND SPIRIT

We are in essence made up of a body, mind and spirit.

This book is principally about our spirit and how it affects the rest of our being and our lives. We have tremendous potential, which is barely tapped. The greatest unexplored horizon for mankind is now thought to be within us and not in outer space. The search for meaning in life and understanding of God takes us to the elusive and even ignored thought of God within us. The Bible and the great books of most religions talk about God being within each of us. "We are the temple of the Lord." So, in realizing our empowerment we are really tapping into our spirits and realizing that this great unknown is the greatest source of richness and answers in our lives.

*Self-Empowerment is
the greatest untapped resource
in the world.*

Each of us can experience this more fully. We can have a better life both from our personal perspective and by making the world around us a better place. It is a natural balance and partnership. We can benefit the world as it benefits us. We are an integral part of the whole. So we believe when we are in our power we only naturally act to create a world that is consistent with our highest sense, our true nature and our God-given talents. By looking inward we can manifest outwardly the best that is within us.

SELF-EMPOWERMENT IS A JOURNEY

Don: Since I have learned these things I have not always been empowered. It has been normal for me to believe in God and I thought I believed in myself. Sometimes I was considered successful by other people's standards, however I was not successful by my own standards. I have succeeded at many things, from being an eagle scout to being a vice-president of a national home building company. I've also done less well and even failed, more because of my empowerment or lack of it than because of my intelligence or ability.

Many evenings I sat on the couch, having another drink, reading books like this, and wondering what was wrong and what I could do to change it. Fortunately, during this time I continued to think and hope and dream my dream. I didn't give up, I got my power back. In some ways I realized that I was still having to prove to people that I was not dumb and was capable.

One of my happiest times was working as a carpenter for eight months, working with my hands and getting back in touch with nature, in Big Sur, California. Why? I spent the first part of my life thinking my happiness or fulfillment came from pleasing other people or living by other people's standards, regardless of the personal cost or sacrifice to me. I have since learned how to take care of myself and do what I enjoy. As Joseph Campbell says, "Follow your bliss."

None of the above accomplishments are wrong. I am still proud of them. But I didn't have balance in my life. In some ways I gave myself away and was out of integrity during these times. I've since learned that I didn't have to be this way. I have great respect for people who do a good job and accomplish things. I now believe we can have greater accomplishments with a more balanced, greater perspective; a perspective that includes being in tune with our spirits.

If you ask three men working on a building, "What are you doing?" you get three answers. One may say "I'm digging ditches"; another may say "I'm building walls"; the third might say "I'm building a temple to honor the greatness of God/man's creation." The third man is the only one that saw his task and accomplishment in a broader perspective.

Chrystol: One aspect of self-empowerment is the freedom to make choices in my life. It has not always been that way. I was in bondage to alcohol and fear. I no longer numb out from life's pain with alcohol but I still wrestle with fearful thoughts at times. Empowerment is not a static state, I move in and out of it. One of my greatest fears was making mistakes, another was fear of change and the accompanying feelings such as panic, a wrenching tightness in my stomach and the emotional pain of uncertainty. However, finally the good news is I can make changes, experience the fearful feelings it brings up and go ahead anyway, believing I can find the courage to risk.

It took many steps and some setbacks before I was ready to make the following change. In 1983 I was manager of an international personnel agency in Calgary, Canada. I enjoyed my job, life, and friends but I wanted to stretch and make some dramatic changes in my life in order to initiate more spiritual growth and strengthen my belief in myself. I planned and gathered information, and decided to move to California with my eleven-year-old son, Trevor. It has turned out to be a wonderful gift to both of us but has not been without its challenges. However, not all my choices have worked out, but probably these experiences have taught me some of my greatest lessons although I wasn't always happy about it at the time. I have heard it said that pain is inevitable but suffering is optional, today I don't choose to suffer. I also believe that God will never give me more than I can handle, but sometimes throughout my life I have wondered.

Don: I've learned, created, helped build homes for people and helped bring energy to the world by helping build power plants and refineries. Only recently have I started to get the point, what my part is in the broader perspective. All of us are creating. Whether it is picking up trash to create a clean environment or teaching young people to experience life more fully.

Being empowered isn't always the easiest of our options. Many of us have wanted someone to take care of us and make it better from the time we were kids. Growing up and beyond this is natural and can be rewarding. It isn't always easy taking responsibility for our actions, safety, and happiness; otherwise we would all be more empowered. Change is scary to us but not changing is even scarier because some things are getting worse in the world around us. We may cling to the status-quo even with its uncomfortableness, its pain, and realizing it may not be working or be best for us. The status-quo is comfortable, it is known, and it is hard to change. Wayne Dyer suggests in his book *Your Erroneous Zones*, that change is inevitable. It's a truism. Now that is the real challenge. Things are going to change anyway. Our families and loved ones fail us at times and aren't always there to care for us. It is proven that our companies will not always take care of us. It's obvious our government is no longer capable of taking care of us (all our needs). Our only true alternative is to take care of ourselves and be self-empowered, through tapping into universal power. If this is truly our only valid choice, the one that won't fail us, the one that works, let's go for it and let's go for it with gusto and passion.

Being center stage in our lives
is the best way to live.

THE PATHWAY TO CHANGE

The first step, of course, is recognition of the need for change; to acknowledge the things that are not working. It's easy to see what's not working in our government, in the lives of public figures, friends, and loved ones. What's not so easy is to apply that critical eye to one's own self. It's very uncomfortable for most of us to admit our own weaknesses and failings. It takes courage. However, courage is a quality inborn in everyone, but sometimes it takes a bit of searching to find it. We all possess it to one degree or another. We all need to acknowledge the courage it takes to make the choice to change. Here are some steps you can make to begin your journey back to self-empowerment.

• Recognize the need to change and that something is not working.

• Recognize that whatever is wrong is a kind of wound that can be healed.

• Identify what are better choices and what your options are.

• Develop the belief that change is possible and that it is your responsibility.

• Recognize that change is an ongoing process.

• Listen to your inner-guide, look at your attitudes and belief systems.

• Act and live consistently with your inner guidance.

• Be open to new directions, risk, and change in your life.

• Recognize and appreciate your successes.

• Share this through your actions so your community and the world can change and be empowered.

PROBLEMS AND OPPORTUNITIES

In the next chapter we look at some issues and injustices we have allowed in our country and world. Although there is judgment, this is not our purpose. If each of us were more involved in what is really going on in our lives and the things around us many of these things wouldn't have happened. We can change for the future, but in order to change something, it must first be identified. Solutions come only after problems are fully acknowledged.

We have given loans to and aided more people around the world than any other country. This has not drained us but benefited us many times over and helped empower us. It is easier to do this abroad than at home. At home we have to admit our own faults, our shame, our own short-comings, our inability or at least lack of effort to solve our problems. This is painful. When we do it abroad we are considered generous, caring, powerful (even if only in our own eyes). Now let's give to ourselves. We need to accept the pain and do what is necessary to take care of ourselves, our homeless, our unemployed, our less-educated, and those needing medical attention. We can do it.

LET'S REFOCUS, REVITALIZE AND RENEW

This book doesn't have all the answers, or even many answers. We are not experts. We present many ideas and suggestions. We can and hope to help make a difference. We can all come up with more ideas and implement them into solutions. Together, all of us can do this and we believe it is possible. It can be fun and joyful in the process. If we choose, we can inspire each other, stand tall, experience our spiritual power jointly and the power of mankind. If we all join together, we can succeed!

2

OPPORTUNITIES
FOR CHANGE

FACING THE CHALLENGE

Part of the purpose of this book is to enable each of us to change and become self-empowered in order to constructively channel our frustration and shame at the condition and apathy of this great country. Its underbelly has been ripped open by political and business scandal and corruption. We have mounting problems of crime and violence, racism, and drugs. We are plagued with government bureaucracies that no longer work, an unjust judicial and penal system, unemployment, inadequate health care and a faltering educational system.

Our government is blocked by its own political process, procedures, and policies. We have a government most of us no longer trust. In the past, our presidents and Congress have put bandaids on serious problems and promised a cure as the patient has become sicker. We have been insulted with election promises that haven't been kept—that couldn't be kept. We can no longer cure declining conditions with bandaid solutions. When candidates come along who seem at last to be willing to tackle the problems head-on, we rally to them in the hope that something—anything—will get done. Meanwhile, as Thoreau put it, we lead lives of quiet desperation.

What will it take for us to act, to rise up from our hopelessness and helplessness? We want our kids to say no to drugs, but what kind of examples are we demonstrating to them with our own addictions and inactions? What will it take to get adults to say no to all the wrongs we see around us? What will it take to get each of us individually to take responsibility for what is going on in the United States of America? We can make the necessary changes and get our power back.

Here are some of the comments from around the country that are symptomatic of people's feelings.

WE CAN GET OUR POWER BACK

In our travels around the country we have heard:

I hate my job but I can't quit because I have my family to support. I don't see any way out. I'm going to be doing this crap for the rest of my life.
— 25-year-old husband, Brunswick, New Jersey

I thought retirement would be fine, but with government playing with interest rates and my almost-fixed income, it hurts. We can't even afford to go see the grandkids.
— 68-year-old retired man, Sarasota, Florida

I keep paying this rent—I've been paying rent for...let's see...for sixteen years—and there's no way I can ever buy a house.
— 35-year-old mother, Phoenix, Arizona

My kids aren't learning in school. What's happened to the schools? We're paying all this money for education and our kids aren't getting educated!
— 41-year-old single father, Tulsa, Oklahoma

I can't walk in front of my own house alone because of the gangs. And that's during the day. At night, no way. I can't go out at all.

— 30-year-old mother, Compton, California

Look at this bill. Look at it! $14,811.00! That's from the hospital. This one's from the doctor ($2350.00). How am I going to pay it? I have $850 in savings and I make $235 per week. I'm not paying it off. I can't ever pay it off.

— 42-year-old female accident victim, Richmond,Virginia.

Do I want a better future? What are you talking about? There is no better future. This is it. I make it here or I don't make it at all.

— 19-year-old male, Harlem, New York

The IRS came in and closed me down. Boarded up my shop, confiscated all my bank accounts. All because I disputed some back taxes with them. How can they do that? What the hell kind of country has this become? Is this America?

— 56-year-old businessman, Chicago, Illinois

Why are so many working families earning incomes below the poverty level?

It isn't right that the only way approximately 10% of our families can survive is with food stamps, welfare, and other aid. Some minorities and youths, who want to work, have an unemployment level that is more than four times the national average. Perhaps there has never been a time in our history when so many Americans have felt their own lives and the world in general to be out-of-control, with no foreseeable way out. Our country is in debt to the tune of billions! We hope the administration and Congress are again planning on cutting our debt instead of accounting manipulations as they have done in the past.

Is our country out-of-control? Do we have any say in our future, in our lives? Will there be any social security when we retire? Our government and justice system are not responsive to our social needs. The government seems to have lost its ability to govern itself, let alone our country, and our justice system does not always provide justice.

The middle class is being squeezed. Young people are earning less, and therefore most are unable to buy homes and don't have the lifestyle their parents did. Teachers, youth workers, social workers, and environmental workers are among the lowest paid, yet their work is among the most important in our future.

*We have to learn to create
meaningful jobs
for everyone who wants one.*

Is our world out-of-control? We are threatened with the destruction of the rain forest, acid rain, and depletion of our ozone layer. We are not effectively handling our waste products, radioactive or otherwise but we still keep generating more. The problems listed above are not insurmountable. We can find solutions.

*Our biggest enemy is our own sense
of helplessness toward these problems.*

We have put a lot of energy into waging war and making weapons. Let's now use this energy to tackle our social and environmental issues with renewed creativity and determination. We also need to look beyond our country and participate as part of a global community.

*There is enough food and resources
to feed and house the world,
yet we aren't doing it.*

Why are people starving all over the world, and why are people starving even here in America while the government stores vast amounts of surplus food? We can solve these problems. By combining our creativity and current resources we can meet the needs of not only our country but also help the world. We can come up with a whole new approach to economics.

Now let's look at how our government affects our empowerment.

GAINING CONTROL OF OUR GOVERNMENT

In 1988, two investigative reporters—Donald Bartlett and Jim Steele—actually read the entire three-million-word contents of the new tax code passed by Congress in 1986. Among other things, they found more than 600 cases in which the authors of that bill made specific tax exemptions for rich friends. For example, there is an inheritance tax exemption for anyone who lived in Tarrant County, Texas, who died on Oct. 28, 1983 at the age of seventy-five, and who had a gross estate of not more than $12.5 million. That particular addition to the tax code came from then Speaker of the House, Jim Wright, and enabled the widow of a wealthy Fort Worth, Texas businessman to save four million dollars she would otherwise have owed in inheritance taxes.

Although the reporters found some six hundred obvious tax exemptions—all favors for rich friends of various members of the House and Senate, they estimated there were thousands of others present that they could not clearly identify because the language of the tax bills was designed to hide both the beneficiary of a specific provision as well as the author.

Millions of dollars in exemptions were given to the rich by the writers of the Tax Reform Act. One of these, Rep. Dan Rostenkowski, D-Ill., actually called it "a bill that reaches into our national sense of justice—and gives us back a trust in our government."

The implications of this story are staggering. Donald Barlett and Jim Steele were not talking about a single infraction in a particular administration, they were documenting an ongoing conspiracy within the Congress of the United States.

There's also the savings and loan fiasco. What happened to Congress and where were the government regulators? Some of them were working for their own interests and against us. So when this happens it's hard for us to trust our government; we need to get our control back.

Another reason that the public is disillusioned with Congress is that some of its rules place members above our regular laws. Members of Congress have exempted themselves from legislation they have passed on civil rights, affirmative hiring, overtime wages, and other laws. In the area of conflicts of interest, the Congress routinely breaks laws that the rest of us have to follow. A specific example of this is in the Lincoln Savings and Loan case where senators exerted influence on the agency that regulates S & L's and delayed action to correct the problem for a substantial period of time. This single case cost us upwards of 100 million dollars, and yet, the five senators have barely had their wrists slapped. Congress's punishment is minimal when its own members break the law or act in an unethical manner.

Our politicians seem to set themselves as a "class apart."

Examples like this are only the tip of an enormous iceberg. However there are areas in our government, which for security reasons, are not a matter of public record. Certain activities of the CIA, FBI, and Defense Department, as well as some delicate trade negotiations and diplomatic activities need to be kept confidential. But national security has become the overused umbrella under which improper actions have been shielded from the general public.

*If the pay, health insurance and
retirement benefits of congress were
tied to what the rest of the country had,
it wouldn't take as long to find a way
for us to have the same benefits.*

Most of us don't have dealings with the government at high levels. We most often come into contact with the government through procedures, such as getting a license or permit, solving a tax dispute or meeting a safety regulation. How often have you tried to work your way through some government bureaucracy and found yourself delayed, and aggravated? Like most of us, you've probably gotten the feeling that many government bureaucrats have forgotten that they work for us, the people. Why should we have to go to such great lengths to satisfy government to operate our businesses? We are inundated with endless regulations, cumbersome and expensive procedures, instead of government being there to help.

*The government hinders our creativity
and even legislates against it.*

When we try to accomplish something worthwhile, for example, to build a desirable facility, we have to go through a multi-year process of environmental regulations, hearings, trials, contests, debates, and delays. A recent case involves a nonprofit organization which cares for our terminally ill patients. The community wanted to build a badly-needed clinic on a wooded site and had obtained all necessary permits to begin construction. A suit was filed, however, to halt the project by an environmental group, which wanted to preserve the natural state of the wooded lot.

Two legitimate, opposing interests were represented here; environmental preservation versus allowing severely ill people to die with dignity. In an earlier time, the community would have held a town meeting and the issue would have been decided one way or the other, or some compromise might have been struck. What happened in this case is that the environmental group was able to use a variety of legal maneuvers to delay the clinic. Ultimately, years later, they received permission to build but at a higher cost to taxpayers and to the Hospice organization. The only winners were the lawyers.

The public has lost confidence in our government, our legal, and our justice system.

In theory, we are in charge of our government and can control its ethics and integrity. Unfortunately, we haven't paid attention to make the government the way we want it to be.

Some elected officials believe they had the right to break the law in order to pursue their own political agendas or personal interests. However there are many dedicated public officials who work tirelessly to be responsive to our needs. With effort on our part we can make appropriate changes. Government can be brought back in line with the needs of our times and its people. As businesses modernize and revamp to stay competitive and responsive to current needs, so can our government.

A Look at Our Judicial System

A friend recounts this conversation in the offices of a prominent law firm.

Client: I never hear the word justice in our conversations.

Lawyer: We rarely ever use that term in our work. Our job is to win cases, and that's what we're good at. That's why we're successful. The concept of justice never enters into our thoughts. We want to win and that's it. Period.

We still call it the justice system, but where is the justice? If wealthy people can hire talented lawyers who keep them out of jail while other people get placed behind bars, where is the justice? If criminals, acknowledged to be guilty, are commonly freed because of legal technicalities, where is the justice? If criminals have more rights than victims, where is the justice?

White collar crime has risen dramatically in our society, and the Michael Milken case shows what often happens when someone is caught. Under the terms of the settlement, Milken, who pleaded guilty to six felony counts and who is serving a ten-year prison term (January 1993 he was just transferred from a prison to a halfway house after a little more than two years in prison), will be left with a fortune of 125 million dollars in his own name and another half a billion dollars owned by his family, according to news sources. His attorneys negotiated this.

This is an outrageous reward for a person who embezzled millions. His investors will have lost approximately 50% of their money because of his actions and it has cost our government millions in that many of these transactions were through Savings and Loans.

Unfortunately, our legal system has gotten bogged down arguing over issues, technicalities, and negotiating deals which really do not provide justice. In one case, a woman had been paralyzed by receiving an incorrect injection while a patient in a hospital. Through legal maneuvering, her settlement was delayed for eight years. For all of that time she didn't have enough money to receive proper care, and her condition deteriorated.

Any time a trial and verdict is delayed
for years
it is inherently unfair.

What has happened to the right of every individual to a fair and speedy trial? Justice isn't served in our system, where we have created a playground for lawyers to make money, waste time and get people off through legal technicalities and subtleties that have no relevance to the case.

Police brutality has received much publicity as of late and it shouldn't be tolerated. But why do we keep excusing demonstrators who throw rocks and fire bombs, and who commonly kick, spit at, and curse the police? Has this become acceptable behavior in America? Is plea bargaining the best way to convict some criminals? Is it ethical and fair to let a criminal go free or get a light sentence because he gives evidence against another criminal?

*H*ave we given up our ethics
in favor of accommodation?

Our laws have grown, one on top of the other, with very few fundamental changes, for the past two hundred years. Few businesses in our country could survive today without reviewing and modernizing its standards and policies every few years to stay competitive. Yet our government has not upgraded its procedures and has become burdened with inefficient and ineffective judicial practices. No wonder so many people in law enforcement are frustrated and de-motivated, seeing firsthand that the system doesn't work.

Where we once touted rehabilitation as a cornerstone of our penal system, now we have given up this ideal and we speak only of punishment and of keeping criminals off the streets. But prisons are overcrowded everywhere in the country, and criminals are getting out without completing their sentences and, sometimes, without ever going to prison at all. Our policy of keeping criminals off the streets isn't working either. What's left? Just punishment? Until we address the issue of imprisonment and rehabilitation in a realistic and positive way, the problems will continue to grow and be a blight and a fear to all society.

America has far more lawyers per capita than any other nation in the world. Have we become a litigious society where people sue at the drop of a hat?

Don: One of the joys of my younger years was flying around in a private airplane, touring our great country, seeing the scenery, taking my friends and having a fun time at a reasonable cost. Recently, it was called to my attention that there are no aircraft manufacturers making small private planes left in the United States.

Why? They have not been forced out of this business because of poor products or foreign competition. They have all been forced out of it because of product liability costs. Liability insurance rates skyrocketed because our courts found the airplane manufacturers liable, in cases, even where the fault was clearly the pilot's or someone else's. Laws that we have passed for the purpose of protecting consumers have sometimes gone to such an extreme that entire industries have been wiped out. How can we "buy American" if American companies no longer exist in many product areas?

Prohibitively high liability insurance is forcing companies out of business; high malpractice insurance is driving doctors out of practice, while high bodily injury settlements have driven up health insurance costs. Yes, people who are injured do deserve compensation, but it is amazing how many people miraculously become healthier after they have won their settlement. Of course, a large portion of the settlements go to the lawyers.

No-fault insurance has been suggested in many states but is still relatively rare. In California, the trial lawyers' associations have fought it tooth and nail because it eliminates their percentages from court settlements.

*Is there any justice left
in our justice system?*

Thousands of people working within the justice system are trying to make it work. Fundamental changes are needed in the system and in our attitudes toward it. It can be corrected.

A PERPLEXING EDUCATIONAL SYSTEM

One of the reasons we are a great country is because we have sought, from our very inception, to make education available to everyone. But now hardly a week passes without some news story about overcrowded classrooms, drugs and violence in schools, the high dropout rate, and uneducated graduates.

Much has been written and said about the problems in our schools. We look for causes but it is hard to focus on any one of them because there are so many bloated school bureaucracies, overworked teachers, latchkey children, single working parents, lack of parental involvement, lack of incentive in students, easy access to drugs, and so on.

We hear that our children do not measure up to students in other countries and we wonder why. As a nation we spend more money per student than Japan, whose students rank much higher. As with so many of our other institutions, this one isn't working as well as it could be. It will continue to be ineffective as long as entrenched interests in education—teachers, administrators, and union officials—continue to resist change, and as long as we, as individuals, do not give it the attention it badly needs.

*Does our educational system
teach limited thinking?*

Many suggestions for improving this are presented in chapter four.

A NEED FOR ADEQUATE HEALTH CARE

We spend more money, per person, on health care, than any other country in the world. Our health care system is not meeting many people's needs - it is not available to some. In fact, we are the only industrialized nation in the world which does not have a medical program that adequately meets the needs of its citizens.

Our government has been debating this issue for twenty or more years. As with so many other compelling issues of our time, the Democrats and Republicans are locked in ideological combat over the types of changes that are needed, and nothing is getting done. Meanwhile, horror stories abound. People continue to become destitute, lose their life savings and often their homes as well, trying to pay medical bills. Large numbers of children are not receiving adequate care. Health insurance is so costly that many families cannot afford it. We have become a nation of medical haves and have-nots—those who are covered by adequate insurance programs and those who are not.

*Congress has voted themselves a
generous health care program
but not one for us.*

Some insurance companies resist paying for preventive medicine because it cannot be neatly cost-justified.

The nation as a whole pays far more in medical costs because of our lack of preventive care. Often doctors prescribe many more medical tests than are necessary for healing in order to protect themselves from possible malpractice lawsuits. Some hospitals buy unneeded, very expensive equipment which is available in a nearby hospital because they are competing for patients. Then neither hospital has enough patients to justify the costs of the sophisticated equipment. So what do they do? The equipment must be used in order to pay for itself, so some hospital staffs order more tests on these expensive machines even though some patients do not need them. The whole nature of the present health care system inherently drives up costs and it will continue to do so until it is fundamentally changed.

Once again, as with so many of our other problems, the nation has become locked into a system that is outmoded and ineffective. Other industrialized nations have solved this problem and so can we.

THE IMPORTANCE OF COMMUNITY

One of the biggest cries in our society today is about the breakdown in families and a breakdown in communities. In some communities people no longer know, appreciate or share with each other. With our increasingly popular suburban lifestyle, many neighbors do not know each other. One of the things that may be disrupting our community spirit and isolating us from others is we don't share our problems; we wear masks and appear successful, happy and doing well, when, in reality, many of us are running scared. We do not ask for help when we need it. How can we expect others to like us if we don't like ourselves?

It was easier to maintain communities when life was simpler. We knew all about the farmer down the road or the local merchant. Their lives were more apparent (other than hiding dysfunctional traits that only the family knew about). We were more willing to be open, share and help each other. In former times, communities were not an option—they were the main thing going.

In some areas we don't know the policemen who protect us and they don't know us. We rarely get to know the men who pick up our garbage because the truck is on a schedule and they can't stop to chat. We no longer get together to build a neighbor's barn—now there are a myriad of building codes with which only a professional builder is familiar. Many don't have a harmonious sense of community or a feeling of belonging.

One type of community is the street gang. We don't have many viable alternative opportunities for these young people. They form gangs to take care of themselves in accordance with the rules of the street. Gangs are a form of community where young people support each other, have common interests and pledge their loyalty. One of the reasons these gangs—these youth communities—are often involved with crime and other disruptions is because we have not tried hard enough to integrate them into the mainstream.

They don't have opportunities for employment and

they lost interest in and didn't see the value of education for themselves. They are a world unto their own, with their own laws, customs, and rituals.

Professional associations are another form of community, at least insofar as they exist for the purpose of the members helping each other. But, sometimes, the true purpose of professional groups has been to protect their turf and keep anyone outside their group from having a say in their activities. Many groups work for the protection of themselves, and not for the benefits of their clients, associates, or other groups. They become contaminated and inbred with their own weaknesses and their own lack of open thought.

A sickness in any part of the body effects the entire body.

Our country has the resources and we can develop the answers. We can work together and make our institutions and traditions work the way they were intended. We have created these problems and we can also solve them. We can work with our leaders and citizens who inspired us to make changes and reach the heights to which human beings can rise individually and collectively. In the next chapter we look at people who make a difference, and see, we still have heroes in America.

3

WE DO HAVE HEROES

WHO ARE OUR HEROES?

From the founding years of our nation, we have recorded the words of heroes.

A government deriving its energy from the will of society...is the government for which philosophy has been searching, and humanity has been fighting, from the most remote ages.

—James Madison

I believe that man's mind is perfectable to a degree to which we cannot as yet form any conception.... Great fields are yet to be explored to which our faculties are equal, and that to an extent of which we cannot fix the limits.

—Thomas Jefferson

Distinctions in society will always exist under every just government. Equality of talents, of education, or of wealth cannot be produced by human institutions.... But when the laws undertake to add to these natural advantages artificial distinctions, to grant titles, gratuities and exclusive privileges, to make the rich richer and the potent more powerful, the humble members of society have a right to complain of the injustice of their government. There are no necessary evils in government. Its evils exist only in abuses....

—Andrew Jackson

What great thinkers, philosophers and moralists have given their best to the history of America! Where are people of this stature today? Who are our heroes in modern America? We have specialized heroes in a very few categories: actors and actresses who win the Academy Awards; Lee Iacocca and others who turn around ailing businesses and make large profits; Magic Johnson or Joe Montana in sports; Peter Jennings or Tom Brokaw at the news desk. Most of us know that Kevin Costner and Jodi Foster have won Academy Awards, but who are our heroes in education, in art, music and literature? How many historians, philosophers, environmentalists, doctors and mathematicians number among our national heroes?

In some Eastern European countries, the greatest heroes in the land are poets. Their sagas tell of the greatness of their people and of the heroic deeds they have done. Poets are held in highest esteem by the entire population of these countries and they are frequently elected to public office, not on the strength of their political skills but on the strength of their moral character. In the United States we have different priorities.

Who are our heroes today?

When was the last time we had a poet for a national hero? On what basis do we recognize heroism, courage, integrity, ability, sincerity, or humility? If we look around, we will see that most of us have built up the wrong kinds of heroes. Many of our American heroes have gained their status by the enormous salaries they have made, by the number of recordings they have sold or by the outrageousness or even the lewdness of their expressions.

How Do We Treat Our Heroes?

We easily idolize people and just as swiftly dethrone them. We seem to enjoy putting them up on pedestals and then meticulously scrutinizing their lives to find flaws. What if we had done so with the great leaders from our past? Were George Washington's taxes, real estate holdings and other business affairs in perfect shape all the time? Or might he have occasionally made some errors— even a downright blunder? What if one small phrase from the Declaration of Independence had been found to be borrowed from an earlier, obscure work? Would Thomas Jefferson have been sued, prosecuted and ultimately destroyed?

What about leaders like John F. Kennedy and Martin Luther King? Are they still heroes or has our investigation of their private lives demeaned them to the point that we have forgotten their contributions? Our media now feel that they can and should discredit a public person's character, regardless of the value of their visions, their leadership or the great things they can offer our country.

What has happened to our common sense and to our humanity? Common sense should tell us that, if we look closely enough, we will find some flaws in everyone. If we continue to insist on perfection, we won't have any leaders left to vilify. What of our humanity? Where is our sense of fairness in the way we treat our public figures? Perhaps most important of all, have we the insight to judge whether a leader is doing a good job, overall? That doesn't mean we have to ignore improprieties, but we don't have to force resignations over some of them, either. We need to return to a common sense, balanced approach when judging our leaders.

There are also heroes among us like you and me. We see them on a daily basis. They are not faces we would recognize, and only rarely do we find their deeds recorded in newsprint or on TV. They are Americans who are not only responsible and honest, they are people who have gone out of their way to do courageous acts. The following excerpt is from an article in the Monterey, California Herald, Tuesday, February 11, 1992, entitled, "Support for S.F. Cabby Eases Courtroom Defeat."

SAN FRANCISCO (AP) —A taxi driver has received a huge outpouring of support after a jury ordered him to pay $24,595 to a mugger he pinned against a wall with his cab.

In May, 1989, the cabby, Charles Hollom chased a mugger who knocked down a tourist and stole her purse. To make sure the man didn't get away, Hollom used his taxi to pin him against a building.

The mugger, Ocie McClure, sustained a broken leg and sued Hollom, claiming he used excessive force. McClure is serving a ten-year sentence in state prison for the robbery.

The protests and funds started to flow Friday morning when popular radio talk show host, Ronn Owens, started "The Charles Hollom Fund" with his own $100 check.

"It's been unbelievable here," Owens said, after receiving hundreds of calls. "The phones are ringing off the hook...and about 95 percent are supportive of the cab driver."

Since the radio show, Hollom said he has been swamped with calls. "My feelings are wonderment," Hollon said. A secretary at Luxor Cabs, Hollom's employer, said that the company was "absolutely besieged with calls. Many of the callers said they would only take a Luxor cab from now on."

What do you think? Was the cabby justified in using his vehicle to apprehend a criminal even if he injured the criminal in the process? If you're like most of us, your answer is a resounding "yes."

In one sense this is a case that has become all too typical in our society. An individual acts unselfishly, with courage, and is severely penalized by our justice system. Thus, among the other powers we have lost is the power to do righteous acts on behalf of our fellow citizens without fear of legal retribution. In the other sense, this case is a victory, because occasionally we citizens get mad enough to do something about injustices. The tragedy is that this happens only on those few occasions when the media become interested in a case and publicize it.

How do the media portray heroism in America? Too often, our main sources of inspiration are radio, television programs and our movies which depict heroism not as courage, generosity or high moral standards but as self-indulgence and violence. One of the reasons we may have lost touch with our heroes is because we have lost sight of what is heroic in our society.

WE CAN BE OUR OWN HEROES

Through our own actions we can be our own heroes. When we live according to our beliefs and follow our inner guides, we are living in integrity. Seeing our nature and our beliefs manifested through our actions is not only empowering to us but to others as well. When our bodies, minds and spirits are in unison we are fully-functioning human beings.

Living by what we believe in is contagious to others and spreads a consistency to the rest of our lives. When we are inner-directed by a consistent and non-contradictory value system, everything becomes easier and cleaner. This brings joy and happiness from within ourselves. We don't need to look for approval from others, which is based on their own values. Practicing and experiencing this will bring us to a higher level of spiritual attunement to our being.

True genius is saying what is in your heart.
—Ralph Waldo Emerson's essay *Self Reliance*

When we listen to ourselves over the opinion of others we will know what is right. Sometimes there will be risks following our own value system instead of the values of others. When are we in our integrity with other people who are in their truth, we together can move our communities and country in the right direction. Many organizations have been started by joint belief systems for a cause. Our problems will begin to be solved when we work together. "I made a difference," "I did what was right by my standards," make us walk tall in our own eyes. When we live to our fullest potential we become examples for our kids and peers which enables us all to be heroes.

There are many examples of people who succeed against great odds. Here is one inspiring example from an article in the *Monterey Herald*, Monday, April 27, 1992, entitled, "Lawyer Willie Gary Didn't Forget."

STUART, FLA. (AP)—Here is Willie Gary's own rags-to-riches, farm-worker to lawyer, philanthropist life story.

Gary's earliest memories are in the fields, joining his mother, father and 10 siblings following the crops as migrant farm workers, sometimes sleeping in tents. In those days, migrants' children were pulled from school at lunch time to go to work.

"You didn't think about things like graduating from high school," Gary said. "I used to question my dad... I used to question the odds. And he'd say, 'Beat the odds'."

He did graduate and a small Florida college announced it was offering him a football scholarship.

"I'd become sort of a town hero," Gary recalled. "First black male child to go off to college from the whole town, in the history of the town. Can you imagine how proud my parents were, my sisters and brothers, the winos on the street, the local people?"

But when he got to the school in August 1967, the scholarship turned out to be conditioned on making the team—and 125 football players received the same offer for the team's 40 positions. After surviving many cuts in the following weeks of practice, he cried when the coach said he hadn't made it.

In that lowest moment, Gary said he vowed not to quit. In desperation, he called his high school coach for advice and the coach as an afterthought mentioned that an acquaintance had just taken the coaching job at a place called Shaw University in North Carolina.

"I'll take a chance," Gary said and caught a bus to Raleigh. He arrived with $7.50 in his pocket and as the university's president said, "a vision in his eyes."

What followed, Gary has retold many times to student groups: how he learned that Shaw's football roster was full and the coach advised him to go home; how he pestered Admissions Director John Fleming every day ("He was determined to get into school," Fleming recalls); how he cleaned up the locker room, unasked and slept on the sofa in the athletes' dorm - until an injury created an opening on the team.

Gary became a Shaw linebacker and a business major. "It was that day I won a spot on the team, but I also won in life," Gary said.

Gary's not shy about crediting his own wits, hard work and can-do personality for making him a millionaire. As a payback for giving him a chance, a U-turn from the deadend poverty of his youth, Gary recently make a remarkable pledge to his alma mater, the small, historically black Shaw University in Raleigh, N. C.

He promised $10 million .

Gary's gift is one of the largest pledges by a black alumnus anywhere and according to William Gray III, president of the United Negro College Funds, it signals a new era of college-giving by graduates who are finally overcoming racial barriers to the accumulation of wealth.

"It's a statement not only about his life and values but it's an extraordinary historical statement about the progress of African-American alumni," Gray said. "Willie Gary is a breakthrough."

This is an outstanding example of what an empowered person can accomplish and his resulting contribution to his university and country.

We need to provide every opportunity for all people to live up to their potential, especially minorities who have more difficulty getting comparable rewards and compensation than white males in our country. Women and racial minorities lag far behind in these areas. Every one of us deserve the opportunity to be our own heroes. We all deserve an opportunity for equal compensation and recognition.

An example of an unsung hero is Dr. Mimi Silbert who founded Delancy Street in San Francisco. She helped more than 10,000 men and women who have spent time in prison reconstruct their lives and become positive contributors to society. Silbert was among six recipients for the second annual America's Awards, sponsored by the Positive Thinking Foundation, of which Dr. Norman Vincent Peale is co-founder. "These unsung heroes personify the American spirit," Dr. Peale says. "They are extraordinary examples of values that make our country great."

"We're coming together to make things happen," Silbert says, "not just with good results but also with a good process. Because life itself is a process. If you fall apart, it doesn't have to end there. Hitting bottom can be the beginning. And I think, right now, that America itself has the same problems that bring people to Delancey Street.

"At one time we all believed we were going up as a country but now we've started to feel like losers. There's a sense of being powerless and an attitude of fear and distrust. We're on the way down. Maybe we have to hit bottom before we can wake up the spirit of hope in America.

"But there's tremendous good in being able to get excited, to believe that rebuilding is possible. Once we know it's possible, we can take the risk of starting again. Then the best part of life is the struggle," Silbert concludes.

In the next chapter we look at ways we think we are empowered. But are we?

4

FALSE EMPOWERMENT

The Quest for Material Possessions

Let's look at some of the false empowering things each of us have. What are each doing that gives us the feeling of false power?

Our lives are disempowered by putting too much value on the wrong things. There are many traps that we fall into which create the false feeling of empowerment.

Our basic values can never be repossessed.

A nice car or a power suit aren't inherently bad, when they are true extensions of our inner values. They reflect our good taste and judgment, when our external and internal values are in harmony.

Don: I have had sports cars, fine homes, a degree, job titles, addictions and illusions of controlling others. These things never really empowered me because I didn't really believe in myself. Now, many years later, I still have some of them. Hopefully, with many hard lessons learned, at least my possessions have become fun. They're enjoyable because, now, I don't need them. My misuse of possessions occurred when I attempted to use them to create self-esteem, rather than to reflect it.

It is a law of human life,
as certain as a guarantee:
to live fully we must learn to use things
and love people...not
love things and use people.

John Powell [1]

On our recent trip to Tibet, one of the things we were impressed with the most was the joy and serenity of the Tibetans. Tibet is a sparse, barren and fragile country now occupied by China, and most of the material wealth is held by the Chinese. The contrast of the vacant robot looks of the Chinese conquerors to that of the Tibetans was phenomenal. Though faced with extreme adversity, the Tibetan people were wonderfully friendly. Their faces radiated warmth while their eyes danced with humor and a passion for living. We felt as though they willingly revealed their spirits in the way they openly looked at us. We communicated in a lively way without language.

Even though their country has been dominated by a foreign power, their spirit is not in bondage and they remain unconquered. What a lesson it was about the importance of the human spirit, and the way we overvalue possessions. The real wealth of the Tibetans and of their Dalai Lama is in their deeply-felt values.

Here at home we have allowed our possessions to become our values. This isn't to say that possessions aren't fun. We can take the results of our work and go buy a car to have fun with it and have exhilarating feelings. We hope we can always enjoy the fruits of our efforts. But these feelings get confused with true power, which is based on self-esteem and our inner values.

A car, home or money do not give us real power, but we can be blinded by advertising and the constant commercial hype. Advertising conditions us, and we may even try to convince a new date to judge us by the kind of car we drive. So we tend to judge ourselves and others by possessions, not by who we really are. How empty we feel when we get caught in this game. We show people all our things but then, when our relationships prove empty, we cry, "please see me for who I am—a human being." Material possessions don't provide human closeness.

PRESTIGE AND FAME—IS IT REAL?

A person can have prestige and fame because of what he is or what he has done. Unfortunately, many athletes and entertainers have escaped into addictions because they have lacked empowerment and balance in their inner selves. There is a substantial difference between being task-oriented versus being person-oriented. A person that performs from inner strength and guidance can be as good, or better, at his accomplishment, than the performer who has only built his life on the achievement of a particular task. We can learn to be a master of a subject and get a degree that reflects our mastery, or we can strive for a degree and lose sight of the learning process and knowledge which is really the purpose of education. One person receives an education which will serve throughout life; another obtains a degree and wonders why it hasn't gotten him anywhere. He may say to himself that it isn't working and convince himself to get another degree and miss the whole point of the education's value.

If prestige and fame are earned because of intrinsic worth and contributions to others, they are a symbol of what really is inside the person; they then deserve it and the recognition will last.

*As we experience our own worth,
it will also be recognized by others.*

ADDICTIONS—WHAT ABOUT AN ALTERNATIVE?

Addictions sometimes give us the feeling of self-empowerment by numbing our senses or shielding us from our true state. Addictions enable us to numb out to the consequences of what we are doing to our bodies and to our lives. The subtle addictions that sneak up on us, where we lose our judgment and our desire to keep our lives in balance can be among the most destructive. Eating is great; too much can be destructive. The same is true with work, play, watching sports, or TV and other things, if we don't keep them in perspective with the rest of our lives. There are baseball widows and orphans as well as work orphans. One of the saddest things heard in many of the support groups is that they didn't know or experience their dad because he was always at work, in front of TV or out with the guys. It's great to have a strong interest or hobby that enhances our lives, as long as it doesn't become an escape from life.

Are we doing some things in excess because we are hiding from other parts of our lives? We can enjoy activities for positive reasons or to avoid facing marital or work problems. As we begin to listen to our inner guides, pointing out the inconsistencies or pain in our lives we begin to experience our true power. Scott Peck says, using slightly different words in, *The Road Less Traveled:* [2]

Life has challenges and problems. If we face them and handle them, we will grow, mature and can be happy. If we avoid them we will stay stuck with these problems.

The use of addictive substances deserves special attention in our country. It is tearing us apart. When half of our major auto accidents involve substance abuse and approximately 90% of the people in our prisons are there because of some involvement with drugs, we have a problem!

The complexity and the magnitude of this problem will require well thought out, long term solutions working on both supply and demand sides of the problem. Also we are fighting a tremendously profitable, illegal, sophisticated business that isn't going to go away easily. A lot of people are making a lot of money.

Individually we can work on solutions for ourselves, our families and our neighborhoods and schools. Not using drugs ourselves and if we can't do this on our own, getting help for ourselves and others can be the first step. Even this is more complex than we can adequately address here. Life, when we're not under the influence or numbed out is definitely better. It takes working on problems that are making our lives painful. Going through the effort to be in our power is worthwhile. We can love, understand, support change, join a 12-step group or a group like Mothers Against Drunk Driving (MADD), and encourage others to take their own steps. Sometimes "Tough Love" and being true to our own values and lives may be a big part of the answer.

The effects of these problems are so great on our communities and our nation that we have to act. Education is part of the solution. Making drugs not profitable or worthwhile for the user are topics we must address.

CONTROLLING AND USING OTHERS

What really motivates our relationships with others, with our familys, friends, business associates and everyone with whom we come into contact? To what extent are our relationships based on real care for others compared to our need to control? Even when we act out of genuine caring, do we keep in mind the nature and real needs of others?

Trying to control others doesn't work. It takes energy to control them against their will. Both lose power. When we try to control someone, we are also taking responsibility for their actions, which we cannot control anyway. Controlling is an illusion. Motivating, on the other hand and working with someone else in their power can increase the power of both.

Letting someone control or manipulate us takes away our power as well. It takes effort and power from the other person and leaves us with feelings of emptiness, impotence and unhappiness.

Making a person do something that is out of integrity in a relationship or employment will backfire and can start a hidden war which is damaging and difficult to reverse. In contrast, two people, each dealing from a position of self-power can multiply the power of both. The difference in energy, enjoyment, appreciation and results can be vastly different. The terms *common cause* and *mutual benefit* do have tremendous meaning when people participate in a cooperative manner.

INTELLECTUALIZING

How many times do we listen to, or ourselves say, a bunch of words and statements about a subject and miss the whole point? Many times two people argue or discuss and they are both very carefully articulating, sometimes profoundly, and yet one party doesn't understand the feeling or essence of the other person's position.

Don: I have been in business meeting after business meeting where all the points have been carefully articulated and a decision made on that basis; but we ended up feeling that a wrong decision was made. There can be a conflict in values that we don't want to address: "He's a minority or she's a woman." Or our linear thinking is too limited to represent what is going on in our intuitive thought process.

Science, humanities, psychology and many fields are realizing that left brain thinking and definitions have limits and can't grasp the full magnitude of what we are capable of with our right brain or whole brain. We can describe an eagle for hours to people who have never seen one and they won't get it (left brain). Yet seeing one for a few seconds will give them a picture they will have for life (right brain).

Some of our intuitive thinking and feelings can't be

reduced to words that will adequately represent the experience. That's okay. It's enriching to become aware that our minds have far greater capacity than the limits of our vocabulary.

One danger of relying solely on intellectual thought is that our underlying values may be ignored. An example of moral versus intellectual values is in the experience of Anatoly Sharansky, the Russian dissident, who spent years as a prisoner in a Soviet gulag.

His captors tried to justify their own behavior and break the spirit of the prisoners by convincing them why their incarceration and harsh treatment were necessary. They used all manner of rational arguments to do this: the prisoners were the parasites of society—they made no contribution; all they wanted was to cause trouble; they were scum who did not understand the lofty ideals of the Communist party; and so on.

The officials who ran the gulag had all the advantages. In addition to weapons, they had good food, good health, warm clothing, news of the outside world and the ability to punish prisoners indiscriminately—which they did. Many of the inmates succumbed, and others, in order to get a scrap of food or a piece of clothing to avoid frostbite, admitted that they were indeed guilty and deserving of punishment.

Sharansky watched the KGB break the spirit of his fellow prisoners. When this happened, they began to weaken and die—their will to live had been broken. He felt his only strength, his only advantage was to cling to his moral sense of right and wrong. The KGB, with their gulags and tormentor guards, were wrong. There was only one way to survive, and that was to constantly remember that moral principle is much stronger than any rational argument.

Our values are the bedrock of our morals and ethics. Although we may intellectually understand that following the Golden Rule is the proper way for us to live, in practice, it is our values that ultimately guide us. When we see someone being wrongfully hurt, it is our underlying values that make us want to help, not our reasoning. This is what causes an otherwise unassuming person to spontaneously jump into a river to save a drowning child.

The use of our intellectual abilities to solve certain kinds of problems is justified and necessary. If we are calculating how much concrete is needed to make a bridge safe, we rely on engineering—not on intuition. But when we get into the realm of human values...for example, how to help inner city youths gain self-respect and a stake in society, then intellect alone is not sufficient.

When we use intellectual thought as a shield or substitute for our basic values, we are experiencing false empowerment which can lead us astray, as individuals and as a nation.

In this chapter we've given a few examples of false empowerment: material possessions, prestige and fame, addictions, controlling and using others, and over-intellectualizing. Other examples include false empowerment through sexual conquest, accumulation of money for its own sake and athletic competition for the sole purpose of proving one's superiority.

False empowerment is anything on which we spend thought, time or money that does not strengthen and reflect our true inner values. In the next chapter we take up the things that really empower us.

5

TRUE EMPOWERMENT

A Closer Look

Why are some people capable of accomplishing great things while others seem to get in their own way? Some people are encouraging and supportive to everyone they meet while others drain away our energy and our confidence. Why do some people see the beauty and exhilaration of life while others are blind to it? Those who have positive accomplishments, who help others and who are, themselves, filled with life are people who have become empowered. This chapter looks at some of the elements which enable us to gain self-empowerment and, by so doing, manifest our best qualities and live up to our full potential.

Self-Esteem

Chrystol: My self-esteem has been so contingent on outside factors that it went up and down like the Dow Jones. Having a good job; a Mr. Right in my life; how do I look—do I need to lose a few pounds. . . These were the issues I was taught to focus on. How I looked was more important than how I felt about myself. I always compared my inside to everyone else's outside and usually ended up feeling not good enough. I should be smarter, make more money; my friend Amanda always looks perfect—how come I don't? Why do I always seem to be with the wrong man? These were my constant concerns.

I just never measured up in my own eyes. I see now how I set myself up in no-win situations. Whenever I did measure up

I'd change the yardstick so that there was always something wrong with me. It was self-defeating behavior. I was taught to see only what was wrong with me. I didn't dare to think good things about myself; that was self-centered and indulgent. In my family, I grew up believing that love had to be earned. So I became a people pleaser, doing what I needed to do to try and fit in although I never believed I did. I felt like a fake which in turn lessened what little esteem I had. It was a vicious circle.

I look back and feel sadness for that lost soul who didn't know what else to do. I believe most of us really try to do the best we can with what we have at the time. I used to fantasize about walking into a store and saying to the clerk, "I'll have ten pounds of self-esteem to go" and the clerk would say, "Sorry, we are all sold out," and I would sit and cry.

I didn't know how to acquire self-esteem so I went to a book store and asked a woman if she could recommend a book on self-esteem. She recommended Psycho-Cybernetics, *by Dr. Maxwell Maltz. This was in the sixties. Since then I have read hundreds of self-help books. Some authors stand out particularly Wayne Dyer's* Erroneous Zones, *Jerry Jampolski's* Love Is Letting Go of Fear, *Richard Bach's* Illusions, *Deepak Chopra's* Perfect Health, *and Sanaya Roman's* Spiritual Growth. *I have read every book these authors have written many times over throughout my life.*

I began to apply some of the techniques in these books, and slowly I began to acknowledge and appreciate some of the good things I saw in myself. I began to believe I was a caring, kind, thoughtful person.

I guess the first breakthrough came when I finally accepted that I am a child of God and I am loved for who I am, imperfections and all.

It has been a long journey building my self-esteem. I know now it's about who I am, not what I do or how I look.

How do we acquire self-esteem? I know it has to do with respecting ourselves. Psychologists believe many people commit crimes because of low self-esteem. They act out by violating society's rules which makes them subject to the penal system. Would most of our prisons be empty if convicts held themselves in high regard? It always seems to come back to the kind of environment we were raised in and the morals and value systems we learned.

We can't go back and change our childhoods, we only have the present to change. There's an old saying: "fake it 'til you make it," meaning act the way you want to become until it is part of you. It's worked for me. We need to take the first step in acquiring self-esteem by starting to act as though we are worthy even if we are afraid we aren't. Faking it helps to change our actions, and when we perform credible actions, they give us confidence so that we begin, just a little bit at first, to really believe in ourselves.

*We are the main character
in our life script,
this makes us the stars
of our own lives.*

OVERCOMING THE FEAR OF EMPOWERMENT

We may say and feel, "I'm great the way I am," which is a way of saying we have good self-esteem. If we hold back an ability or trait because of fear or a mental block, we will not experience our full empowerment. Our empowerment increases as we grow in the process of life. We may hold back because it can upset the status quo of our lives and can be a threat to others. Wouldn't it be scary to start doing things that threatened our partners, our bosses or our friends? They may say they like us better the way we were.

Embracing our power can be terrifying, because we will have the responsibility for our own lives. However, we have the power within us and also the guidance and connection with whatever we need to pull it off. Even though we try, we can't really shrink away from this anyway. Knowing that we can be lead and empowered to the extent we need, makes this realistic, less fearful and the only satisfactory way to live. We will grow to this level in increments, it won't come all at once. Life when lived openly is a series of growing experiences. We will get through pain and struggles and experience more joy and live our lives with more abundance.

Many relationships have been threatened by one person experiencing growth and the other not. The optimum relationship exists where all parties are encouraged to be all that they can be. This sets up some new dynamics both threatening and positive, but the enrichment of life for both is worthwhile.

Throughout our lives we change, and from these changes we gain new insights, new experiences and new power. This is far better than stagnation.

*We can only be responsible
for our own happiness and power
and not that of others.*

In employment the same principles are true. If we don't grow there are less opportunities for advancement, excitement and enjoyment in what is a major portion of our lives. Some of these lessons have come the hard way from foreign competition or from someone else getting a promotion or a job we wanted. Being all we can be is satisfying and it also raises us to a new level of understanding and expectations. "Will I like this new level and can I succeed at it?"

Success comes naturally to us
when we follow our inner guides and
are in integrity with ourselves.

Changing doesn't mean that we have to give up our previous way of life. We can still have the same friends and the same enjoyments, but will be experiencing them from a higher level.

A story, as old as stories themselves, teaches us about this: "I was standing on the edge of a cliff, seeing the magnificence of life before me. But I was scared. Someone pushed. I went over the cliff and I soared." Our new and greater experiences can enrich our lives and those around us. With openness we will grow, appreciate and thrive at new levels.

Don: At times in my life I have vegetated in front of the TV or in a book for the purpose of numbing out instead of enriching my life. It's comfortable, it's safe, it's restful. Most of us experience a form of "burn out" some time in our lives but numbing out can be replaced by focusing on replenishing. We sometimes develop habits to avoid too much stimulation or new experiences. I have found that a better alternative is to open to the enjoyable revitalizing things around me. I replenish my energy by enjoying flowers, beautiful scenery and experiencing nature. Sometimes a walk or vigorous exercise will take away unsettling nervous energy better than alcohol or other numbing agents temporarily do. It is wonderful and elevating to rejuvenate ourselves from the abundance of nature and life around us. We also need some times alone and some times together to enrich our lives and lead us to new levels of empowerment. *A Course in Miracles* states, "We will never be challenged above our abilities."

Let's choose to expand and grow.

A Turning Inward

Don: As we talked about in chapter one, every major religion suggests we all have a higher self, God within us, a spiritual self. In the past when I heard some of these things, due to my upbringing I believed that God was outside of me so these thoughts were sinful. I turned off my thinking and openness. It was fine for me to pray, but it wasn't okay for me to meditate. I considered that visualization practices or affirming something I didn't have but wanted was stupid.

Gradually, my inner yearning to grow and experience more, overcame my rigid labels. If we can be open enough to try some of these in addition to prayer, we may discover their effectiveness and the feeling of rightness they give. This alone demonstrates their validity. If we try this we will learn that they are just different names for the same thing.

When I began to try these kinds of exercises, which are

outside of traditional religious practices, I discovered that I don't need to limit myself by thinking about things in restricted ways— that the experience of visualizing or affirming is every bit as valid as traditional prayer.

Prayer is a kind of meditation
and
meditation is a kind of prayer.

Traditional western systems teach us to think of religious concepts like God, prayer, grace, heaven, eternal life, salvation, etc., in defined and limited terms. We have been taught them by teachers or learned from books and some of us have not made them our own. We haven't confirmed them by our own direct experiences. With meditation, visualization, spiritual healing, communication with inner guides, or any of the nontraditional practices, we can know to what extent they are right for us. Let's not limit them by defining them. Let's keep open and powerful— as broad as our varied experiences make them—and not limit them by our thinking and our vocabularies.

Praying, meditating, visualizing and affirming on a daily basis empower us. All of these practices need to be done with an open mind, a sense of thankfulness and the ability to let go of control. The degree to which we are able to say "Thy will be done" is the degree to which our inward-turning practices will be effective.

A friend told us of an experience in Hong Kong, some years ago, when Billy Graham was on an evangelical tour and was giving one of his rousing sermons in a large athletic stadium. The crowd must have numbered 25,000-

35,000, mostly all Chinese. While they were Christians, most of the people in the stadium didn't understand English, so there was a translator that stood right next to Billy Graham.

Graham spoke in his sonorous tones, waving and gesturing to make his points. He spoke of surrender; surrender to a power much greater than ourselves. The translator waved his arms and gestured in an imitation of Graham's movements but the inflections of his spoken Chinese were so different that the effect, to an English speaker, was very humorous. Toward the end, Graham shouted, "Do you want to be saved? Will you accept Jesus Christ as your personal savior?" and he waved his arms dramatically, his Bible clasped in one hand. The translator dutifully repeated the questions in Chinese, shouting and waving his arms, also with a Bible in one hand.

Our friend related that after the sermon was over, and the people were leaving the stadium, they all had a glow about them, a sense of peace and contentment that he had not seen before in their faces. He thought about this for some time...about being "saved" by Jesus through the medium of a Chinese translator, and he finally concluded that the language didn't matter, what really mattered was that they had surrendered. They had, at least momentarily, given up control of their lives, given responsibility for their destinies to a greater power. "Thy will be done."

Don: There was a time in my life when I seemed to need the TV on or music on wherever I was or no matter what I was doing. I have noticed when I have stayed with friends or particularly with some young people, they turn the TV on and do not pay attention to it, or put their walkmans on and go about their business, whatever it is. In cars they always have their stereos blasting. There is no quiet or silence in their lives.

Much of my inspiration and internal communication comes to me when I am quiet. When I don't have my mind busy with noise and am leaving an emptiness in my thinking, new thoughts, daydreams, answers to questions and spiritual insights come to me. Again, if we are busy or full all the time, new information or insights don't have an opportunity to come in.

It is important that we give ourselves the gift of being open to what is available from within ourselves which includes messages from our inner guides. We need to have time that is uncluttered, uninterrupted and not full of noise or activities. We need to spend some time alone, it is a form of meditation. We can listen, without an agenda. We will be amazed at what we hear and what becomes available to us.

*We have richness and answers
beyond our wildest dreams
right within ourselves.*

Miraculous things can happen when we let go of our ego control and surrender to a higher power within us. Turning inward (listening, asking for what we need through prayer, visualization or affirmation and, finally, learning to let go) is another element that leads to self-empowerment.

IDENTIFYING OUR PASSIONS

What are we passionate about? Do we feel the essence of ourselves much of the time? Do we block out our feelings? How long has it been since you have thought about what you really want to do or allowed yourself some frivolous or simple pleasure? When was the last time you watched a child play or saw a beautiful flower and felt warm inside? The essence of life is experiencing ourselves, others and all of life.

*All things start with an idea,
can then be made into a vision.
Action can follow.*

We are all given unique gifts, talents or interests. Some of us have blocked these out of our conscious thinking so we are no longer aware of our passions. Do we have a gift for being an architect or musician, or a passion for sports? We may have been told we should be a lawyer instead of following our interest in painting or some other area. We don't need to drop where we are in our lives but we can reintroduce some of our old interests back into our lives. We can even change careers or where we live. Experience your feelings and passions. Do something with them, even if only in small ways.

DEVELOPING AND TRUSTING INTUITION

Miracles happen everyday. A self-centered grouch

stops to help an older person or a little child. A very busy "type A" person stops going ninety miles per hour for a few moments at the sight of a sunset. These shifts occur in all of us if even for a short moment. Whether daydreaming or appreciation of a person or nature, times of reflection are treated with suspicion and apprehension in our predominately linear society.

It's okay to have a feeling for someone, but we better be able to back it up with analytical thoughts of their strengths and weaknesses so we aren't surprised or vulnerable to their actions. This is particularly so if they work for us or if we are dependent on them or their actions in important business dealings or personal areas of our lives. Our lack of ability to understand or be comfortable with our feelings, makes us vulnerable in business and in life. Can I trust his actions? Is she being truthful? How about me? Am I a good manager? Am I in control? Am I a good motivator? Do I read situations and people correctly?

Can we acknowledge that many of our best decisions are made intuitively?

How do we rationalize our analyses and how do we justify our decisions and our actions? We do it by finding logical reasons that support our actions so that we can approve of ourselves, and be considered rational and astute by others.

Sometimes we do all the right (logical) things and it still doesn't fly. Then, after all our normal thoughts we wake up the next morning with the right answer. Where did it come from? Maybe we got a flash of brilliance. Or when the burden is almost too great and unbearable, a feeling of peace comes over us and we know it is going to be okay, even though we don't know how. If we start to think it through, we start to panic again.

What is this part of us that we don't understand, this source of insight, knowledge or knowing that doesn't fit in with our linear, analytical thinking? Do we trust it? How do we use it? How do we have it as part of us and balance it with our western style of thinking? Can we appreciate it and understand it with our linear minds?

If we look at the experiences and thoughts of people whose actions we revere, we notice that there is a commonality of experience. They felt a feeling and were led by it. Something came over them or through them that we have difficulty understanding and especially talking about.

This type of experience has been given several labels, such as insight, inner-guidance, intuitive reasoning, right-brain, universal mind, spirit and God's knowledge or will. Any of these labels limit and define it as less than it really is. We are back to a box or label that limits us. Yet in our society, we feel that we have to define it in order to understand it and to communicate it adequately and fully to ourselves and others.

An appropriate expansion of our thinking may be for us to learn to appreciate and accept something that we don't fully understand.

If we look at the actions of our heroes and what made them heroes, we often hear something like this: "I just visualized it and then I painted it as I saw it." There is a universality to this source of greatness and inspiration. Seeing and appreciating this is not negating our thinking process, but is becoming aware of a larger perspective or a more whole picture of our being.

How do we think? Here's how *Webster's New Collegiate Dictionary* defines two parts of our thinking process:

Intellect—The ability to reason or understand.

Intuition—The immediate knowing of something
          without the conscious use of reasoning.

Our temptation is to try to make the comparison clear, precise, complete and final—to think of intellect and intuition as clear opposites. This saves us from the burden of having gray areas, of staying undefined and indefinite. We want to place thinking in boxes so we are more comfortable with them.

Our other labels for mental abilities are couched in terms of opposites as well: we have left-brain and right-brain thinking, linear versus non-linear, thinking versus feeling, limited versus unlimited thinking, structured versus free thinking, and closed versus open thinking.

Some of these ways of describing thinking have hints of western versus eastern culture. We even include time in our quest for clear distinctions, so we have thinking in the now and thinking in the past or future.

Our need to categorize things as opposites includes

good versus bad, right versus wrong, yin versus yang and introvert versus extrovert. But if we are really open, don't we find some of both sides in any of these pairs of opposites? In any situation there can be right and wrong on both sides. We all have both introvert and extrovert traits in varying degrees. This doesn't suit our need to label or categorize but it more accurately represents real life.

As an example an aeronautical engineer, with his technical understanding, knows that it is theoretically impossible for bees to fly. The size, shape and movement of their wings can't provide the lift to support their body weight and their complex in-flight maneuvers. However since a bee doesn't know it "can't" fly, or it is refuting the principles of aerodynamics, it does its thing, and the engineer is forced to ignore this apparent contradiction of knowledge and fact.

We are all bees at times in our lives. Against all logic we find ourselves flying.

Don: My career and life have been filled with accomplishments that many people thought were impossible, such as building a complete manufacturing plant in four months. These kinds of accomplishments happened because I didn't know they were impossible, and because people believed in me, humored me or even said "It can't be done—let him fall on his ass." You too, can probably think of things you have done that have amazed yourself and others.

Some of us have had similar successes occurring in our childhood or in fields we knew little about, because in these environments, we didn't know or weren't told that it couldn't be done. In performing beyond the probable, we called upon an ability above our normal knowledge and limits; and each of us actually became a greater person during that time. We may have also used our knowledge or linear thinking in the process, but a dream, a vision, an inspiration or a knowing of something without the conscious use of reason enabled it to occur. Michael Murphy's book, *The Future of the Body*, gives many examples.

The downside is also true. We have failed at many things because we and others believed we couldn't do it. When you read about Einstein, Edison, Lincoln and other heroes, they have had the same ups and downs. Their accomplishments have happened only when they were inspired, or had the vision or dream. Lee Iacocca was thought by Henry Ford II to be inept, incompetent and undeserving of the presidency of Ford Motor Company, yet he reversed Chrysler's impossible position and became a hero to many. Same man, same abilities, same resume and the same linear facts. But his confidence, his inner guide and his vision made it happen. This deeper part of ourselves, which we find hard to define, radiates to others and can be a tremendously powerful force both positively and negatively.

We are a part of the entire living universe, and there isn't much that we can't do as part of this life system. When we or others tell us that we can or can't do something, both outcomes are possible. Our knowledge, our education and our abilities are very important to our success but only when accompanied by the power, the belief and the inspiration of our nonintellectual side.

Learning not to limit ourselves to previously defined boxes is one of the master keys to success and happiness. We can all open up to our limitlessness with some work and with a deliberate change in our thinking.

One of the best judges of whether we are on track is how we feel within ourselves. It will feel good when we are right on. When we are centered and have our power we will know it. When we don't, we'll feel uneasy, we'll feel ourselves pulled in different directions and we will experience dis-ease.

Sometimes we will seem to hear conflicting voices or feel pulled in many different directions. The question is which one is right, which one is our inner guide?

Our inner guide may be the quietest of all of them. Following its lead will give us the most inner peace and an empowered and balanced life. Other choices may be a pulling toward what you were taught as a child or by your parents, "You shouldn't do that." A person close to you, such as a wife, your children or someone special, may try to convince you that what they want is what you want. There are many forms that this manipulation can take, from "you should . . ." to "don't you want . . . ." These messages may even come to you non-verbally. They are often subtle, and through repeating become reinforced. These then become recorded and are stored in our subconscious as voices (tapes) for a long time, from many sources.

These voices also surround us in our society. Advertisers: "This car will . . . ," employers: "You must do this for your career . . . ," or our government and others try to convince us to believe things.

Look at all your choices carefully and if possible, in a peaceful frame of mind. Don't be rushed. The best answer can come through. This gives you the best possibility of knowing what is right for you. Some of these answers come a little at a time or in steps. That is why we say our life and spiritual growth is a path.

We may change to something that isn't right for us in the long run but it can be an interim step. This can prepare us and open us up for the next step when it comes, so we will be ready. Some of these indirect steps may feel like they are a mistake but in general have valuable lessons to teach us and are what we need. Some of us get to where we need to be by a longer more indirect path than others. The lessons along the way will be valuable to us and may be enjoyable as well.

Allow your choices to teach you.
They can be the source of
your greatest learning. [1]

We believe that our intuition is a part of our inherent spirituality. We are born with this spirituality. We can and do experience it, as do many of our heroes. We can understand and develop it, and if we learn to use our own innate intelligence and creativity that springs from within us, we can be our own heroes.

INTEGRITY

Don: Much of my life I have let others determine what I

should do, what I should be and how I should act. Parents influence our education or careers, both directly and subtly. Bosses, our employers, friends and family encourage and can manipulate us into directions that don't always seem right to us. This can only be done with our permission. Yet in looking back on my own life, I have gone on many tangents and in directions that weren't right for me. Sometimes we realize it, sometimes we don't.

Integrity means being honest with ourselves and others, and being consistent with our thoughts and actions. If it doesn't feel right to us, we probably shouldn't do it. It's important to think it through, process it, and be right with ourselves.

Lying, cheating, hurting other people or ourselves, or being out of integrity takes away our power. Beating and blaming ourselves unduly for what we do to ourselves or others takes away our power. Forgiveness is vital. When we're not honest with ourselves, we become torn apart or ill at ease. We have dis-ease, get sick and diseased. The benefits of being in integrity far outweigh the liabilities.

For too long we have played games
we don't enjoy
by rules we don't believe in. [2]

We have to learn how to change, to apply this simple, direct principle. Being responsible for ourselves and not others is a good start. Looking at the truth in ourselves without beating ourselves up moves us in a direction of consistency. It is far less painful and brings more pleasure to follow our internal truth. It brings our bodies and minds into harmony with our hearts.

If we're right with ourselves,
true to our values
and consistent with our spirituality,
we will have more power.

Seeing our nature and our beliefs manifested through our actions is not only empowering to us but to others as well. When we state what we intend to do, we let people know how we will act. By being consistent, we let others plan their own actions accordingly. When people or government say one thing and do another it is impossible to respond accurately.

A SENSE OF BALANCE

There are many areas of balance we need to examine in our lives. We need to take care of ourselves first versus the priorities of others: loved ones, family, friends, employers, our community, country and the world. We have to be true to ourselves or nothing else works. Our integrity and the value system we live by needs to be followed or we will pay a price in conflict and dis-ease. This is balance. Beyond this, there are times when serving others serves ourselves best. When we take care of our family, we take care of ourselves. When we do a good job for our employer, it protects our job. We can only show our love or other intent through our actions. Keeping true to ourselves will guide us in proper balance in relation with others.

If we have a disease in one part of the body it affects the entire body. So we can't just eat the right things and ignore exercise, health habits, thinking, safety or even relationships outside ourselves. Taking care of our bodies, minds and spirits requires balance.

What we do with our time, effort and creativity is an area of balance where some of us get into trouble. Addictions and obsessions upset balance as well. Balance does not mean equal emphasis on each facet of our lives, rather it means not neglecting areas that are necessary for our well-being.

Serving others is usually of benefit to ourselves and others. Some very creative and talented people give a large percentage of their lives to a cause—from which we all benefit. The truly healthy ones have time for varied activities and experiences.

In most cases if we occupy our time with one obsession and don't have time for anything else our output and enjoyment of that obsession will be lessened. Nothing can thrive and do its best in isolation or in a situation where it isn't balanced by interaction with other parts of life.

We are not isolated beings nor are our actions isolated. We are a part of nature. Balance is not only a weighing of two forces but it is a flow as in the shedding of old to create the new. Life and death are synonymous in the cycle of nature. By observing the balance of nature we can learn how to balance our own lives. We go through difficult times to learn and to develop the ability to make our lives better. When we look at bad experiences in light of what we can gain from them, all of life has balance. Truly, our most despairing times stimulate periods of growth, understanding, and insight.

SPIRITUAL AWAKENING

*Spiritual awakening is
the most essential thing in man's life.*

—Kahlil Gibran [3]

Chrystol: I see spirituality as a very personal belief pertaining to the soul. I started my spiritual journey as a child going to Sunday School. Although my parents didn't attend church, my father being very British, thought it was important to raise me as a Christian in the Anglican Church. I was both reverent to the point of piousness and irreverent to the point of skipping some Sundays and spending my offering to buy a chocolate ice cream cone and reading comic books at the drugstore. However, my Sunday school teacher was very kind to me and took an interest in me outside of the church activities. I was able to trust her a little and she helped me to believe in God, which planted seeds that have spiraled into an ever-increasing appreciation of God and our world. Even trying to define spirituality somehow limits it. I experience it as my connection to God.

For many of us, spiritual awakening is a process and not an event. My process was like the prodigal son's in that it was a long way home. My path led me into alcoholism in my late twenties and early thirties. I continued to pray but I felt I had lost my connection. It was not that I felt God had turned away or deserted me, but rather I no longer felt worthy of His love. I was losing control of my drinking, although not enough for the man I was married to at that time to suspect I was an alcoholic. I knew I was losing the battle. Alcohol had me, I no longer had it.

There seem to be no coincidences in life and I was given a copy of the autobiography of Bill W, the co-founder of Alcoholic Anonymous by a friend I traded books with. I identified not with *his personal story but with his feelings and knew if I didn't get some support I would end up being like my parents, something I swore I would never be. I joined a 12-Step program and I believe that was one of my spiritual awakenings.*

I share with you the following poem I wrote in January of 1977, six months after coming into the program. It tells you where I was and had been.

Redemption

I feel an enveloping sadness and try to turn away from
   the pain of yesteryears and even today
My thoughts are woven in complex strands that encase and
   strangle my long protected heart
That was afraid and hidden away, safe, from reaching out
   and daring to seize the love, warmth and tenderness
   I know exists
I feel the hurt deep within me cry out for release from
   the closed chamber where it lies dormant and then
   erupts when its restless slumber is disturbed
I taste the bitterness of anger and resentment of some
   past or recent and sometimes imagined offense
The disillusionment of my shortcomings and failings that
   at times impede my growth and also tend to make
   me look and challenge the imperfections of my
   fellowman
Tears of frustration and self-pity stain the porcelain of my
   facade
That is so carefully polished for those to gaze upon
   and remark
"How calm she is"

Sometimes this observation is indeed true
At other times, my emotions are twisted and distorted,
raging in unchecked riot within the caverns of my
consciousness
Screaming for numbness to block out reality, so I may
not experience in varying intensities, feelings I
will not admit exist
And when at last, weary and drained in the aftermath of
my holocaust of unleashed fury
I can rest awhile, bathed in sunlight, the dark shadows
fleeting from my face
I feel the hand of God in mine and once more find peace
—Chrystol Lucas, January 1, 1977

This was followed by my poem of celebration seven days later.

Rapture

I am on the threshold of untrespassed worlds that are
unfolding before my wondrous eyes
Now is the time to set aside my apprehensions and rush to
embrace life, unafraid of what may lie on the eve of
tomorrow
Looking in childish anticipation to what the day may
disclose
Warming to the unexpected smile of a friend, the touch of a
reassuring hand
Letting me know I no longer face the world alone
Not anymore like the chameleon, ever-changing and
adapting just to abide

Shedding the camouflage of shielded emotions that can
     now be revealed without trepidation
Free and uninhibited to rejoice in being only what I am
My spirits soar to the pinnacles of my own sensitivity
Longing to bring within me life's secrets and to retain
     but a single moment of first awareness
To dwell upon and cherish in quiet solitude memories
          that enrich my soul and give sustenance to carry
     forth into each day with gratitude

— Chrystol Lucas, January 8, 1977

Wayne Dyer puts it very beautifully and succinctly in his book *You'll See It When You Believe It* — "I am a spiritual being having a human experience rather than a human being having a spiritual experience." [4]

INTIMACY

The main thing in life is
not to be afraid to be human.

—Pablo Casals

Intimacy, for most of us, is a process of moving toward life when we feel safe and moving away from life when we feel threatened, fearful or misunderstood.

Chrystol: For me, to be intimate is to be vulnerable, to risk telling you who I am in the innermost recesses of my soul. My beliefs, feelings and values are in the open and it's very scary because I fear being judged. I need to trust before I can be intimate. It takes tremendous courage to risk and be intimate. It's usually a process of getting to know another person and feeling comfortable and safe enough to not just share who we are but our dreams, joy, humor, our child-self. It also seems hardest to share my shadow side: the anger, disappointments, frustrations, depression and self-pity.

Due to the emotional wounds of growing up in a alcoholic environment, with violence and rage almost daily, I was left with a legacy of fear, loneliness, abandonment and neglect.

For years I never really trusted anyone and this included myself because of some of the decisions I made in life that emotionally and physically devastated me. In relationships I always chose emotionally unavailable men and took jobs that were disappointing. I was either over-qualified or under-qualified. I kept putting myself in no-win situations. I had very little self-esteem and because I couldn't trust myself I really didn't trust others. There wouldn't be as many divorces if it were that easy to be intimate. We need to be intimate with our children so they can see us as human beings not just in the role of mom or dad. We need to show our humanity in all our relationships.

This poem was an effort to reveal more openly who I am:

Reflections

My life is like a chalice, spilling over, receding,
    constantly replenishing and ever changing
I wish to know others but fear to reveal myself
My face does not betray loneliness for am I really ever
    alone
Or do you look into eyes that are filled with unwept
    tears
Are turmoil and frustration hidden under the veneer of
    disciplined calm

The scars of the past are deep and remain proof of
     bygone anguish
My mistakes weigh heavy upon my breast
At times I long for yesterdays I wish I had changed but
     did not
But then again, my compromises have been made
I must live only for today
So instead I escape into other lives and deny my own
Strangers and friends look to me for comfort and
     guidance
I give what I can only to wish it was more
And try to ease the misery in lives that are etched
     with sorrow and confusion
I look outside my own pain to help those closest to me and
     yet seemingly unable to reach, although their need is
     great
My heart in my outstretched hand waiting for some
     sign of recognition that will enable me to lighten
     the burden
My voice is unanswered and I must again search for
     justification for my existence
Each time I turn I hope the encounter will hold the
     answers
Like sunlight dancing through a prism, elusive with
     no clarity, but with a promise of fulfillment
But once more the illusion is short-lived and slips
     through my fingers like quicksilver
Knowing all the while the key is within me
     I have wisdom but I am a contradiction to myself

Momentarily, I catch a fleeting glimpse in my mind's eye
of the mosaic of my being
I am a dreamer brought to earth by reality

—Chrystol Lucas, January 29, 1977

Most of us are not creatures of isolation. We long to connect and fear it at the same time. We share ourselves through laughter, tears, writing, talking, work, hobbies and play. How much and how deep we share depends on the level of intimacy we have established in a relationship.

It is empowering to be intimate with others in our sharing and it strengthens our sense of who we are. Perhaps we need this mirror to appreciate ourselves more, otherwise we would be living in a vacuum. When I don't share and need to, I seem less to myself and I feel rather vague in defining me to me. I guess I just feel more real when I share who I am. I can risk standing up to be counted, allowing you to see my humanness without the masks, showing the flaws and knowing I am still lovable.

When we build walls to protect ourselves, unfortunately we also wall out the good stuff. When we share, we can take little steps and consider it the beginning in building the bridge to another person. Opening up to others will transform our lives; it certainly did for me. I feel I am still not as open as some, but when I began it was like stepping into my life. I had always felt on the outside looking in through the window of life. Today, through sharing, I finally feel I belong.

This poem is one of the small steps that helped me get to know myself. I had spent years running away from who I thought I was. I have carried this poem in my wallet for fifteen years and read it whenever I lose a sense of myself...which I might say has been very, often.

It is rewarding to find someone whom you like but it is
    essential to like yourself
It is quickening to recognize that someone is a good
    and decent human being, but it is indispensable to
    view yourself as acceptable
It is a delight to discover people who are worthy of
    respect and admiration and love, but it is essential
    to believe yourself deserving of these things
For you cannot find yourself in someone else
You cannot be given a life by someone else
Of all the people you will know in a lifetime, you are
    the only one you will never leave nor lose
To the question of your life, you are the only answer
To the problems of your life, you are the only solution

                —J. Coudert, 1977
                Montreal, Canada

COMMITMENT

Commitment—to bind or obligate
as by pledge or assurance
            —Webster's Dictionary

Just the definition alone strikes fear in the hearts of many of us who have been commitment-phobic. People are waiting longer to get married, even into their thirties and forties. The survivors of the divorce wars are waiting longer before remarriage or choosing to live together. They are afraid another marriage will fail.

*Commitment is giving my all to
something
and being open to
all it can give me.*

We are in a changing society that is changing faster than most of us are able to keep up with. Also, many are just opting out of marriages and relationships permanently; they feel the risk is just too great.

In the past, in their careers, employees accumulated up to thirty and even forty years with one company. Now the average tenure in a clerical job is one-and-a-half years. A new college graduate is expected to change careers seven times in his working life. If we don't make a commitment in relationships or jobs, we feel it won't be as painful if it doesn't work out; the sense of disappointment, loss and failure won't be as great.

Chrystol: For most of my life I was afraid and committed to very little. Even in my first marriage my hand was always on the door, ready to leave if there was more emotional pain than I could handle.

Looking back over my life, I have made two major commitments. The first was to my son, Trevor who is now in college. For most of his life I was a single parent. In my mind, he came first. Many days he was the sole reason I kept going. I couldn't do it just for myself—I just didn't have enough self-esteem. The second major commitment was to stay sober one day at a time through a 12-Step recovery program. Just about everything else was subject to change...a job, relationships, the places we lived.

In my upbringing, "looking good" no matter what was happening was what life was all about. If I made a commitment I couldn't keep or a wrong choice, how could I save face? So my automatic response had been "I'm fine, thank you" even if I was dying on the inside. For me, commitment was a living death.

Today, for me, commitment no longer is an intimidating concept. In fact it's just the opposite. It feels good to be able to trust and have faith. I can commit to growth, to spirituality and to integrity. It empowers me by allowing me to give my all to my relationships, however I choose to be involved.

I opened a personnel agency in Carmel, California in 1986 and it has weathered some tough economic times. It's now 1993 and it's doing well. I enjoy the business, but even if it changes I have lived up to my commitment to make it work.

I have also learned to change my mind when something is no longer viable. That doesn't mean it's a failure—it means I am now able to re-evaluate it and decide whether or not to make another commitment.

For me, now, commitment is no longer something to avoid; it is an option I can freely choose. When I choose to commit, I am enhancing my own power and self-esteem.

We can all begin again, starting each day.

GROWING OLD—MATURING?

There is a tendency as one gets older to pull back and be conservative. This is healthy, normal and protects us from trying to do things our physical bodies are less capable of doing. Skiing down advanced slopes may be exhilarating to an 18-year-old, challenging at sixty and dangerous at eighty. It may have been fun to work out at twenty but it can be work to even "fun out" at seventy. To some seniors, walking five miles or traveling is fun; to others it's work and more trouble than it's worth.

Don: In Eugene, Oregon I met a woman well into her seventies (naturally she wouldn't tell me her age), having her 30-foot-plus, motorhome serviced. She regularly travels alone around the country, towing a car, when she is not spending time in Washington or Arizona, her two regular residences. Three months earlier she had been in an accident, destroyed her motorhome, then bought a new one and was on the road again. She was very proud of the fact that she took up skiing at seventy and could still bike ride on 25-mile trips with people half her age. She was young, vital and exciting to be with.

In Alberta, I met a couple, both nearing their nineties who traveled seven months out of the year in their car and tent trailer. We had a delightful, stimulating evening together.

Another friend, sixty-five, bicycled through Europe for a week during two summers and he still skis.

My mother, in her late seventies, rode dunebuggies with me, went para-sailing in Mexico, and traveled half way around the world to ride camels and elephants and see her grown children in Europe and the Mideast. She remarried and enjoyed many more years, swimming twice a week until a couple years before she left this world at close to ninety.

We've all heard of Colonel Sanders, the founder of Kentucky Fried Chicken, and Buckminster Fuller—they had great lives after sixty-five.

Maurice Chevalier was asked at one of his concerts where he performed over two hours with only a short break, "What do you think of being seventy-eight?" He replied, "It beats the alternatives."

Our bodies and minds change with age but according to some experts, more changes occur with lack of use than from age itself. Attitude affects our abilities and enthusiasm for life more than anything else. So how do we enjoy a full life as we gain years? Continue to be open to new experiences. Take some risks, especially those kinds of strengthening risks like daring to be different, and being your own person, which aren't as risky when you are older. Most importantly, stay center stage in your life. Don't give responsibility for your life to others. Sure it's great to delegate and have help, but we stay young to the extent we are involved in our own lives.

We are spiritual beings with minds and bodies.

Our spirits don't age. The people we've talked to who are young at heart and are really enjoying life have a peacefulness, a centeredness, an enthusiasm for life. If we listen to our inner guides instead of people telling us we are old, we can experience a communication with life and nature that only maturity brings. Many can set and change their priorities and experiences each day because they don't have the demands of a job or raising kids. We may have less days ahead of us (with our bodies) but each day can be lived more fully and in the moment.

There was a time, in our culture, when elders were respected. That time seems almost gone. We can't bring back the days of yore but there are some things we can do to regain respect for our elder citizens. One of those things is for each of us to do our utmost to continue to grow in self-power and wisdom as we mature.

With age, it is more important than ever to listen to and appreciate what is really important in our lives. We have a lot to offer ourselves and the world when we keep an open, inquisitive and flexible attitude. The mature years can not only be good years—they can be great years for ourselves and for the world.

6

EXERCISING SELF-EMPOWERMENT

BEING OPEN

*Much of what we experience
is filtered by our perception.*

We only see what we allow ourselves to see. Reversing an old saying, Wayne Dyer expresses it well with the title of his book, *You'll See It When You Believe It*. This is one way we limit ourselves and lose our power. If we only see what we are open to, and only believe what we want to believe, we may be really limiting ourselves. For example, how many of us have held beliefs about our parents from childhood only to discover, as we become adults, how wrong we were?

When we talk about people or objects, we tend to know them by the limits we put on them and define them by where they begin or end and what their main traits are. Yet many are much more than our limited perception of them. When dealing with other people, for example, we tend to focus on traits that we don't like, and our narrow focus prevents us from seeing the good in them.

"I don't like him," we say. Yet if we make the effort to look at some of his good qualities, a different image emerges. "I don't like my job," we say. Yet that job may be where we need to be right now or it may be the best we can get with our present frame of mind.

When we see something of beauty, do we limit our experience of it? Perhaps poets and artists are able to create with real openness, without surrounding themselves with boxes more than many of us. Reading or viewing a creation of a talented artist often produces a great appreciation and a sense of reverence for the work. Somehow, something came through as energy or as an experience beyond words or beyond the limits of the artist's brush.

We have all experienced the change in feeling in a group when someone enters a room. Everyone's energy mystically changes for better or worse, and yet we can't put our finger on why it happens. We have a negative effect on the people in our lives and on our kids when we come from a bad day or bad experience. They can just feel it. On the other hand, when there is something exciting to share happiness literally flows in a way that we can feel tangibly.

Labels and limits attach themselves to us from the time we are too young to remember, and continue to affect our everyday lives. We learned some of the most damaging subconscious programming of our personal "tapes" when we were children:

- You're bad.
- You're stupid.
- You can't do that.
- All you ever do is lie.
- You're really dumb.
- You're always going to be...
- If you do that I'll punish you, fire you, etc.
- How come you aren't working, doing your homework, etc...?
- Do you want to fail?

- If you do that, you don't love me.
- If you do that, I won't love you.

These and others limiters have had varying effects on us. We have been restricted by others, and we have limited ourselves and bought into many beliefs that are untrue. The needs of others, their manipulation and projections, have done a number on each of us.

How many times have we been told that, "the computer won't allow...," "it's company policy that..," or "the boss or Mom says...," as if these edicts have been cast in concrete. Better not fight them and don't question them—they're sacred.

We do have choices! Astonishing!

Don: A few years ago I spent a full year traveling around the country. I found that many people who had left behind their habitual situations and normal routines were living quite well in ways different from my own. It was shocking. Some worked seven days a week and some worked only two days a week.

I met some people who had given up high level executive careers to work in a hotel in Yellowstone National Park for half of the year, and fish and enjoy nature in their off hours. The rest of the year they spent doing other things they enjoyed in another part of the country. These happy people became self-motivated and followed what was right for them instead of blindly obeying what others, and what society, considered appropriate. Many of them had less money yet were far richer in their lives than before.

True joy is found in doing what you love. [1]

LIMITED AND UNLIMITED THINKING

The classic problem that illustrates limits in thinking is the one that asks you to connect dots with straight lines. Note in the following that nine dots are arranged in the form of a square.

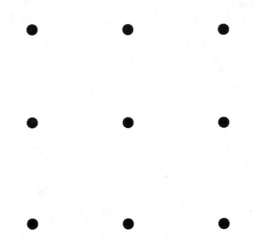

The object is to connect all the dots with four straight, continuous lines. You can start anywhere but you can't lift your pencil off the paper once you have started. Work on this problem as long as you want. After you're finished, turn to page 110 for solution.

We limit our thinking in many ways. We don't think of possibilities for other employment or richer lives, sometimes, until our industry slows down or we are laid off. There are many ways we can enrich our lives with less limited or more limitless (unlimited) thinking. "I can't afford it," or "I'm to old," may not be true at all when we put new possibilities in perspective. People have told us they couldn't take a desired trip or a class to study a subject of interest to them. But when the cost of other things in their lives or the time spent on other activities that were far less important to them, was compared they saw how ridiculous their limited thinking or old habits were.

When we look outside our self-imposed limits we come up with better answers.

A company's stated problem may be different than its real concern. "We have too much inventory," may really mean: "Our sales are down," or "The cost to warehouse and to maintain our inventory is too high." Another terrifying example is: "We have to let you go because...." While management's perception (of being staff-heavy) may be sincere, the real problem may be caused by poor market penetration, incompetent management, or any number of problems other than too many employees. But because we are used to looking only within our limits, we often fail to see the real causes of problems.

Communicating Fully

It's easy to communicate superficially. "I'm fine thank you. How are you?" One of the biggest challenges in getting along with others is knowing what they are

Answer to problem: Looking at the example below, the solution to this puzzle is easy if you don't restrict yourself to the confines of what you think the problem really is. No one told you to restrict your lines to the borders of the square—but chances are good, you just assumed it. This illustrates our frequent approach to problems in our lives—we limit our own thinking.

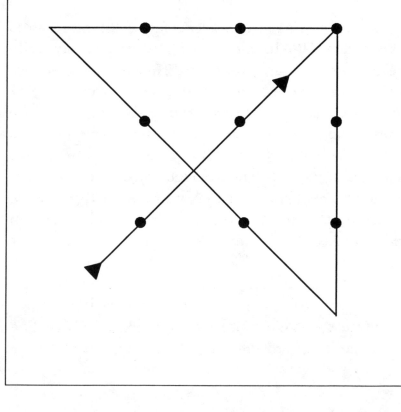

thinking—really thinking. Sometimes we don't want people to know what we are thinking.

We can all remember times when we thought that we didn't understand or didn't know what someone meant or we didn't know how important something was to another or felt misunderstood ourselves. This often leads to a frustrated sense of futility. Then, of course there are times we purposefully veil our thoughts and feelings, intentionally hiding them from others. Although this may be a means to gaining a legitimate advantage, as in negotiations, we sometimes can set up a condition of language hide-n-seek or one-upmanship that ultimately impedes any real communication.

Our vocabulary and language are only one of our communication tools; maybe the most limited. There are many ways we can improve this facet of our communication. Of primary importance is listening. Are you really listening, are you hearing and are you hearing with empathy? What is he trying to tell you? Are you getting feedback when you are talking? Is she hearing, is she understanding what you are trying to convey? Are you thinking of what you are going to say next, are you thinking of something else or are you really trying to grasp the full essence of what he wants to have you understand? What is your filter system or translator changing or blocking out? If we look at this honestly, we may find many judgments clouding our ability to really hear another. These are all things we can work on to make better communication.

What we do deliberately that makes us less than fully

present during a conversation is important to acknowledge and understand. "She talks so slow. I know what he
is trying to say or I can read her mind. I have too many
other things to think about or do."

We once heard that an air traffic controller can hear up
to nine conversations at a time and actively think about
and participate in several. This is hard to conceive. In
most effective communication, one person is speaking at a
time and it is important that we pay full attention.

One of the first things we need to do in conversation
is to make up our minds about how we are going to
participate. The importance of the person and the subject
are determining factors and this can change without notice
in the middle of a conversation. The best focus is listening
to hear, feel their message and understand, not to respond
or try and fix the problem. Also when we're not actively
listening, it shows and it sends a stronger message than
anything that is said.

> *We have a much greater intuitive sense
> and have perception
> far beyond word communication.*

True communication begins beyond discussion of
numbers and facts. No matter what is said verbally, our
emotional and body communications have a language all
their own. Our bodies may transmit fear, anger, resis-
tance, nervousness, a sense of flirting, like or dislike and
other messages without the use of words. When body
language and emotional cues don't agree with the words
being spoken, it's a sure sign of hidden agendas.

Animals readily pick up unconscious messages. Many people have trained themselves to read these far more subtle feelings and energies. Being "psychic" is really about having highly developed faculties for registering subtle energies, including the ability to "see" energy cocoons or auras around all living things.

Don: I studied massage therapy to learn to communicate more fully with people. Often times, particularly with Chrystol, I can sense where she is tense, or in pain, how her energy is or even what is wrong or what she is thinking without verbal communication or touch.

Most of us can develop these abilities. Some think we are the most advanced creatures on earth, yet many other species communicate accurately and in tremendous detail without a language we can detect. It leads us to the premise that our written and spoken languages may be very crude while our other ways of communicating may be far more advanced than we realize.

Let's communicate with the full essence of our beings.

Our body language and feelings usually give us away, so wouldn't we be better off having our words say what we truly feel? Admitting that we can't fully explain in words how we feel may show tremendous wisdom and insight.

Many of our communication problems come from holding back what we really think. This plays tricks on people and keeps them from trusting their intuition—they hear you saying one thing but they are really picking up something else. Holding back information can cause many problems as shown in the examples below:

Action with No Communication	False Conclusion
A man has fears and problems so he becomes moody and withdrawn.	His wife may think he is having an affair or some other incorrect assumption.
A woman becomes withdrawn because of her health and chooses not to discuss it because she thinks it reflects on her femininity.	Her husband may think that her withdrawal means she doesn't love him anymore.
A teenager may become listless over a boyfriend or grades.	A parent or parents may suspect drugs, health problems or any number of things.
An employee may become less productive over a family problem and he is embarrassed to share it.	The employer may conclude that he isn't dedicated or hard working and is just goofing off.
Parents could be uptight and fighting over finances or other matters.	Their children may conclude that there is something wrong with them; that they are to blame or there may be a divorce which will cause the loss of their home.

There can be thousands of variations of these types of misunderstandings. Being open and honest has its consequences but the benefits far outweigh the liabilities. In seeking the truth we aren't making assumptions and forming wrong conclusions. More than one war and one divorce have been caused by not knowing the truth and assuming something else. If we delve into our feelings, we become aware of the despair and lack of power from not knowing the truth. Hearing or being told something that doesn't jive with our feelings or perceptions sends "doesn't compute" signals to our internal computer. Changing to open, honest communications causes some fear but it's better to hear the truth and be able to live in integrity and with full understanding.

*Communication with our spirit
is ultimate communication.*

As we become more adept at communicating, we become more sensitive to subtle communication. In the beginning, subtle communication means listening beneath the words, understanding body language, and so on. But as we improve our listening and hearing skills, we can begin to apply them to the most subtle forms of communications—those understandings we gain through prayer, meditation or listening to our inner guides. Spiritual communication is the ultimate communication.

COOPERATION

We can't sabotage or be indifferent to a good relationship and expect it to benefit us. We also have to take care of the people and entities that take care of us. If we don't help our employers succeed, we weaken them and lessen our value as employees. We need to take enough interest in our government so that it functions in the way that we want. As individuals, we are part of larger entities, whether these are family, community, company or government. They don't do well when they are ignored. We need to get back to taking care of the things that are important to us, whether it be our own selves, our relationships or our country.

Japanese competition in the auto industry has made it necessary for Americans to quit the traditional fighting between employees and employers, to be productive, innovative and take care of what we have. The result of this, according to some statistics and many articles, is an upturn of interest, of pride and of job satisfaction. It helps all of us, individually and as communities, to be a part of an effective working organization that produces a quality product.

We are in a rapidly changing world and cannot stop progress, nor should we. We can help guide it in the direction from which we can all benefit. Change, openness and growth are among the best experiences in life. We need to be open and prepared. Fighting ourselves, our organizations, our government or the hand that feeds us doesn't give anyone power. We can participate in making ourselves, our associations and our environment better. Redefining our definitions to allow more freedom and opportunity can seem risky, but is ultimately more fulfilling. The interesting part of change is that it is inevitable;

so we have the choice of fighting, or participating in it and helping it grow in a direction of our liking.

Healthy Relationships

Unless you love someone,
nothing else makes any sense.

e. e. cummings

Society is based on people cooperating and meeting each other's needs. There is a whole array of songs about "People Who Need People," and "As Long As He Needs Me." Our lives have meaning and purpose because of others in our lives. "No man is an island." We are enriched and get feedback from others whom we enjoy in our lives. This enrichment can be enhanced and our lives become fuller when there are no hooks or unfair conditions in our relationships. We feel good when a person is with us because they want to be. It's scary when we know that, sometimes, they won't want to be with us when we want them to be. This is the starting point for manipulation, trade-offs and guilt feelings in our lives. "I won't leave him because I don't want to hurt him," or "She can't take care of herself"; "I'll love him as long as he does this or that"; or more directly, "If you do, or don't do that I won't love you or be with you."

It is a necessity to have freedom
in healthy relationships.

We have fear when we think a person only acts a

certain way because of the negative consequences to them. We begin to have self-doubts when our own feelings of not wanting to be with someone lead us to realize they may have similar thoughts about us. If we feel we lose in a relationship, or can't stand for a person to act the way they want, then the negative traps get set up. There will always be both negative and positive factors in our lives. There will always be trade-offs. The threat of losing our job, getting hurt or losing a loved one can motivate us to change our actions positively.

When we take the attitude, "If you hurt me I'll hurt you," we both lose. We are concerned with losing rather than gaining, being or enjoying. If we ask others to give up a day of doing something they want to do in order to be with us, there is likely to be a negative feeling that will affect both. If the other decides they want to give up their activity to be with us, than we both can have joy and our power.

Unfortunately, in many of our relationships we give away our power when we don't feel we should. We also figure out ways to take away other people's power to get what we want. What happens is that we end up with a lot of win-lose or both, lose situations and poor compromises in our lives.

When we are in a relationship because we want to be, and encourage the other person to be all that they can be, we usually benefit from their positive energy, their creativity and insight. This free and open exchange of our power brings the relationship more power than the sum of its parts.

Many of us have felt the power of creativity and warmth of our kids when we haven't held them back, and have seen their spirits soar. Unfortunately, the opposite is true also, and many young people have felt robbed of their joy and enthusiasm for life. We have passed this from generation to generation because of fears, rules or customs we have inherited. These are the things that we can look at and change. We can form a new wholesome pattern and force in our lives. When we follow our inner guides and don't try to control or manipulate or be controlled or manipulated by others, our experiences can be magnificent. When we see the best in people, and in ourselves, we experience the best.

Learning to Enjoy Living

If we believe we have only a choice of A or B, Yes or No or This or That, we severely limit ourselves. Our choices are much more than hanging onto this job or that job; they can include self-employment, a long vacation and many different lifestyles and means of support. Our choices can be open, wide and varied.

Don: Only now am I realizing in my own life that freedom is not gained by saving money, accumulating possessions, owning insurance or controlling other people, which are all just efforts to feel secure, or even the security of having people close to me. They can all be lost in one incident that we call a disaster. Freedom is leaving things open to new experience, where people can be with me because they choose to be, where my security is within me and my opportunities are constantly opening up before me. Now I try to experience life to the fullest rather than having things own me and being worried about whether this investment will go sour or that will go wrong. I'm not saying you should give up all responsibility for yourself. On the contrary, I'm saying take responsibility for being alive and open rather than having excessive concern for security only.

When I quit working for a large company four years ago I traveled around the country and experienced people who were living far happier than I was on less than $1,000 a month (a fraction of what I was making), doing exactly what they wanted to do. The thing they all had in common was that they had given up clinging to their fears and their pasts. The book *Do What You Want and the Money Will Follow,* by Marsha Sintar, has many good thoughts on alternative lifestyles and following your dream. It's amazing how many people are plodding through their lives without enjoying themselves. Enjoyment comes when we begin to make our own choices, out of love and interest and our innate desires to create and live, and not out of fear for what we might lose.

*Life isn't a dress rehearsal,
this is it.*

TAKING CARE OF OURSELVES

The type of care we are referring to here is taking care of ourselves in relation to others. We are not responsible for anyone else's actions. Yes, by being inconsiderate and irresponsible we can cause pain. By being considerate and responsible we can improve the lives of others. But we cannot be responsible for another person's unhappiness, for their abuse of drugs or alcohol, for their failures at their jobs or at not taking care of their own lives. This is sometimes very painful for us to hear and experience with our loved ones. Being true to ourselves, living in integrity, being honest with others and also caring is the best we can give in our relationships.

For ourselves and others,
we are responsible
for doing the best we can.
We are not responsible for the results.

Knowing our own boundaries and making sure they are healthy are ways of taking care of ourselves. Not being taken advantage of, having our kids responsible for their own actions and being responsible for our actions...each of these enriches our lives and our power.

In addition to having given our power away in close relationships, we have also given it away to our government and our employers. It doesn't work to blame companies and blame the government when our careers become obsolete, our companies and industries slow down and our jobs disappear. We can all improve our education, become knowledgeable in other fields, save money for a rainy day and our retirement. We can have a fuller life and be more self-sufficient, independent people because of our looking out for ourselves and empowering ourselves in this way. Taking care of our resources, whether in the form of a home, money, job skills, family, health and loved ones is primarily our own responsibility. Not our employer's.

Not our government's. No one's but ourselves. Doing this can have an extremely rewarding and empowering effect on each of us.

*Enjoyment comes when we begin
to make our own choices, out of love
and interest
and our innate desire to create and live,
not out of fear for what we might lose.*

It is our inborn nature to look out for ourselves in a healthy way. Healthy love, caring and respect can only flourish in an atmosphere of mutual independence. Dependence, whether on loved ones, friends, employers or government makes us less powerful, less free, less happy and less able to uplift and bring out the best in each other.

A vital point in taking care of ourselves is to identify and shed the old habits or traits that no longer serve us. Introspection and listening to our inner guides lead us in the direction of growth. To take in something new we first have to make space for it. When we're busy with old habits or old relationships which no longer serve us, we do not have the time or energy for developing healthier, more appropriate new ones. There is an example of a person who was very busy with many problems who went to see a wise monk for advice. The monk poured tea and listened. After awhile, when the guest's tea was half gone the monk poured tea and kept pouring until the tea ran over the top. The man pointed this out and the monk acknowledged that he was right. The point he was making is that only when we empty ourselves sufficiently to provide adequate space can we take in something new. Our lives and bodies are constantly shedding the old to be replaced by new experiences, relationships and new cells. We need to make room for new in our lives.

Some people live or push themselves in a way that they feel burned out and therefore want to numb out. Repeating what we have said before, when we numb out with drugs, alcohol or TV we are ignoring the signs to replenish ourselves and take in new energy. Relaxing in front of the TV can do this, but taking in the beauty of nature, running or taking a walk or having enjoyable times with people may be more revitalizing. There are times we are tired and we feel like relaxing or numbing out, but let's think about or do something to rejuvenate ourselves. The universe all around us is constantly renewing. Let's participate and partake rather than destroy ourselves.

HONESTY AND FORTHRIGHTNESS

When problems arise between individuals, within a business or in government, people often avoid being direct. One of the reasons for this indirectness is that we feel telling the truth will offend others. But, in fact, telling it like it is, sincerely and without malice, allows people to cope with the problems. We need to learn to be honest and handle the consequences. Our families and friends have shied away from truth and directness to save face and not offend us. We all deserve true feedback so we can deal with problems as they really are. It's much easier to cope with the facts than something we might guess at because we aren't told the truth.

There are those who purposely manipulate or hide information in order to protect themselves, or project a certain image. We are told things regularly that just plain aren't true. It might be a politician who has just been elected, telling his constituents he won't raise taxes even though he is already planning to do so or knew it was impossible to live up to his promise. It might be a boss telling an employee everything is alright when he really intends to fire him in the near future. A restaurant we know of closed down on Christmas Eve, without any warning, and when the employees went to cash their last paychecks, they bounced. Some "Merry Christmas."

It might be an implied message by our advertisers showing that if we drive a certain car we will be surrounded by attractive lovers. It's our nature to want to believe people. Yet this lack of integrity by so many has made many of us disillusioned or cynical.

Our whole society has become accustomed to being dishonest about why we do or don't do things. We have gotten so used to being indirect and not offending people that we deprive each other of honest feedback which can help us realize how our actions are affecting others. This lack of directness also occurs because of our fear of being sued, or of our desire to avoid the "mountain out of molehills" syndrome.

Lack of forthrightness
has been institutionalized
in our society; it can be changed.

So often we make excuses that aren't true when we turn someone's request down or don't want to deal with them. This fear of the consequences leads us to make all kinds of excuses when we really mean that their product or service or personal characteristics aren't satisfactory. How can they learn and improve this way? On a larger scale, our society is prevented from improving because so many people do not know why they have failed to get a job or obtain a contract, etc.

Let's get direct.

This lack of truthful integrity is so widespread in our country that it affects everything from adult relationships, to our kids, to politics, to government and even to international relations. Somehow we've gotten to the point where we think it is okay to lie to our parents, our kids, each other, our employees or employers and even ourselves. Sometimes our government lies to us, our elected representatives hide the truth from us. Our government doesn't tell us what or why they are doing things when it affects other parts of the world.

It is discouraging to realize the things that have happened because of our lack of truthfulness. Our kids don't trust us with taking care of their future, and we don't trust our government, even up to the highest levels. We are engaged in one big cover-up. No wonder we don't feel good about ourselves or our country right now. We have gotten numb from lack of honesty and integrity. Knowing the truth about what is really going on is empowering. We sometimes do this in times of war or other national emergency where we combine our efforts and accomplish great things. Sometimes, we do it in the workplace. We also need to do it at home.

With honesty
we can live life head on.

REFUSING TO ACCEPT WRONG SITUATIONS

The following story illustrates the consequence of accepting wrong situations.

I was driving through San Francisco where I witnessed a terrible auto accident. An elderly woman drove through a red light in a busy intersection. She didn't notice a motorcycle crossing the intersection. I watched in horror as the motorcycle and rider rammed into the side of her car. The rider was thrown into the air and landed some twenty feet away on the pavement. He was wearing a helmet but the impact was so severe he lay unmoving, his legs twisted into a grotesque position.

After he had been carried into an ambulance and taken away, I and several other witnesses described the accident to the police. A few days later I made inquiries and found out that the young man had survived—barely—with a broken back and pelvis, multiple fractures of his legs and serious internal injuries. His lower body would be completely paralyzed, with no chance of his ever regaining use of it. I learned that he was twenty-three years old, married, with two toddlers. He had been an auto mechanic.

I heard nothing more about the accident for two months and I assumed that all claims were being settled without my being called as a witness. One morning, an insurance investigator came to see me. He was representing the woman driver's insurance company. She had claimed that the motorcycle driver was at fault and the investigator had come to see if he could get a witness to corroborate her story so they could get a judgment against the young man.

I asked the latest news of the young man's condition. He told me the medical report stated that the victim was permanently paralyzed and he had undergone many more operations. He would probably not be released from the hospital for another six months. I asked if the woman who was the cause of the accident had been to see him or his wife. The investigator replied, 'No, we strongly discourage any contact with opposing claimants'. A few minutes later he left.

That really bothered me. I suppose there is merit in keeping insurance claimants apart after an accident. After all, the injured party might try to murder the other one. But what would have happened if that woman had seen firsthand the pain inflicted on the young man; if she had seen the face of his young wife at the hospital, day after day, month after month; if she had seen the little children and realized that she had forever deprived them of a normal father—if she had seen any of that and if she had any feelings, could she have allowed her insurance company to try to place the blame on him? [2]

Each of us has probably heard some variation on this theme. The principle is that we know, we feel, that we have a responsibility to our neighbor; but the law says, no, we don't have a responsibility to our neighbor—we have a responsibility to follow our lawyer's advice. We don't talk to the injured person and we don't apologize or try to make amends. We have been seduced into accepting a rational argument (let the lawyer handle it) in place of human decency and caring.

Don: I know of a divorce where one party allowed her attorney to make false statements and inferences which changed the settlement substantially in her behalf. This had tremendous affects on her kids and ex-husband. When questioned, she said "I couldn't help what my attorney did."

There are many things in our lives that we are involved in or close to that have tremendous impact on other people. Can we really come up with a disclaimer, that we can't or couldn't help it? Think of the accidents that happen after one more drink or drugs, or people who are killed by weapons we produce. We can be responsible for things we do and participate in. These are some of the steps, little and big, that can make a difference in our lives and world. There is so much harm being done by our looking the other way. Let's live by our value system instead of copping out in wrong situations.

BEING FLEXIBLE

Some lawyers like to claim that our greatest attribute as a society is that we are a "nation of laws not men." By this they mean that only through impersonal, objective laws can we maintain a just society. When laws are taken to extreme and people, as individuals, dismissed, then laws are no longer just.

We have lost sight of the purpose
of our laws
and spend too much time involved
with legal technicalities.

We have all experienced lack of regard for people on an individual scale. On a larger scale, we recently read about a local Hospice chapter being denied a zoning waiver which was needed to build a facility for the care of terminally ill patients. Its lawyers filed for the zoning waiver five minutes after the legal deadline.

The Hospice was unable to obtain the needed zoning waiver and thus could not proceed with building. State funding which had been contingent upon receiving the waiver was then withdrawn. Matching funds from a private foundation which were contingent upon receiving state funding were also withdrawn.

"It's the law!" stated the planning commissioners who denied the waiver, "We have nothing to do with it." Yet practically everyone in the community wanted the badly needed facility: the public, the planning commissioners, the county supervisors, the state funding agency and the private foundation all wanted this project to go ahead. Isn't this stupid? A good cause has been thwarted by a legal technicality.

When we feel our family or friends or we ourselves

are being treated in an impersonal way due to arbitrary regulations, we can politely suggest to other people involved that the rules need to be flexible enough to accommodate human needs. When we read about the night stalker, a serial killer or child molesters in preschools, who get off charges or have years of delay in trials and cost tax payers millions of taxpayer dollars, we all have responsibility to take some action to correct these injustices.

> *Laws must be kept current to serve people, not the opposite.*

We are graduating more lawyers than engineers. Are they working to make laws and procedures more simple and able to serve us or are they encouraging the further complication of an already inflexible, cumbersome legal system? It will take each of us expressing our views in these areas to get changes made by our representatives. It can be done. It's appropriate to say again, that if a private company functioned the way our government or legal system did they would have been put out of business a long time ago.

It will take considerable time and effort to reverse these trends in our society but, individually, each of us can contribute to doing it. We need to have a system which is flexible and changeable enough to work efficiently for us.

RATIONAL RISK-TAKING AND GROWTH

Life is a risk. We have many risks daily and throughout our lives. When we drive down the road an oncoming car may cross the road and hit us head on. Hundreds of times a day we survive and ignore potential risks. A friend of ours has been through bankruptcy twice and is a multi-millionaire for the third time. Each of us are open to different kinds and levels of risks in our lives.

Babies fall many times in learning to walk. They try time and time again. If we leave them alone they will learn. If we praise and encourage them, they will learn it faster than if we scold or tell them to be careful and demonstrate concern over each fall or mistake. Risk-taking is natural to our nature but as our life progresses we take fewer risks. Much of this is good, some of it isn't.

*The more we can be open
to new experiences,
the more we grow and appreciate life.*

Have you noticed that the more we do and experience, the more we are capable of doing? By seeing and appreciating life and growth in those around us we can learn and apply these principles in our own lives. We can look at setbacks and failures as learning experiences. Every time a baby falls we don't call it a failure to accomplish walking. Fortunately, he doesn't give up and learns a little more and tries again.

Motivate yourself by your dreams, wishes and aspirations. Look at others who succeed and use them as models. If they can do it, so can you. Learn, get informed, become an expert or proficient at what you want. Visualize you are already there or doing it and it will become real to you.

*Broaden your perspective and
eliminate your limits;
the risks will be minimized.*

Much is said about people losing homes and jobs, and having serious problems during our lean times. It is good to remember there are options far beyond the ones we allow ourselves to think about. We just came back from a trip around the world where in many locations the average person earns the equivalent of $60 a month or less. We as outsiders can live well and happily with a complete family in many locations for way under $300 a month. Putting things in storage, cutting your losses, and living in Bali or other parts of Indonesia, or Mexico or other parts of Latin America, is one possibility. We're not proposing this but all of us have options we don't even begin to think about. It is important to do some of the things of which we have always dreamed. When we follow our passions, we will be energized and will have a much greater chance at successful lives.

Many of the things we think we need in life may not be true. Look at the things you have that you haven't used in the last year or five years. When was the last time you really looked in your closet, your garage or basement? What does it cost and how much space does it take to keep them? There is beauty in simplicity.

Friends of ours sold a very nice home and now have two nice mobile homes in locations they hadn't even thought about a couple of years ago. They spend enjoyable time traveling between them in their recreational vehicle.

They do this, all for much less than the cost of living in their one previous home. This was all scary to them and a risk several years ago; now it is a delightful reality.

Many careers, industries and locations don't suit us or have the opportunities for us anymore. This forces us to change. Taking a risk can be the best thing that ever happened to us. When we do it wisely, with all our knowledge working for us, risks and growth can provide a wonderful new lifestyle. We can combine all of the above in a balanced way. We don't have to throw away all of what we have learned and done so far but rather use it as a basis for new and exciting growth.

Our opportunities and experiences are limitless.

THE EFFECTIVENESS OF SELF-EMPOWERMENT

At times we all work above or below our abilities based on what motivates us and how we view ourselves. We are also affected by what employers and others say about us. When we are in tune with ourselves and our power, the sky's the limit, both insofar as what we can visualize and what we can accomplish. We can soar like eagles. The actions of Joan of Arc, Einstein, Edison, Michaelangelo and others are examples of what a single human being can accomplish.

Self-empowerment is multiplied by numbers. In 1992, less than 1/100th of 1% of American citizens prevented the House of Representatives from covering up who among them habitually wrote bad checks. The cover-up was in motion; it had been decided on and yet we stopped it. Hooray for us ordinary citizens. We have power, and it takes only a bit of it at the right time to do great things.

We can create change.

We also have the power to disempower ourselves. An executive, an athlete or any individual can do tremendously well and then become de-motivated and not be able to perform even basic functions. The balance between greatness and creativity and insanity and incompetence is very precarious. Messages we receive that cut us off from our spiritual selves can cause us to become non-performers. People who do well have good habits ingrained and don't let external circumstances de-motivate them or make them lose sight of their own personal truths. They also don't let internal messages or old tapes sabotage them. Being centered and knowing where real power comes from makes a difference in what we can accomplish.

Sometimes, there can be a subtle loss of our power through agreements and negotiation. Particularly in politics we have allowed a special favor here and there, thereby losing sight of the original intent of the issue. This is how we all give up our power. We have let government, churches, countries, friends and families create and implement standards that may not be fair. We then accept these unfair standards. For example, company policies that do not respect the dignity of the individual are wrong but we very often go along with them for fear of losing our jobs or future promotions. Even when laws are fair as written, they are frequently enforced unfairly—sometimes accidentally but often deliberately.

To get our power back
we have to look at who we are.

We need to look at our feelings, our doubts, what works for us and what doesn't, what makes us feel good and what doesn't. Is there a better way to feel about ourselves, a way that fits us better both internally and how we project ourselves to others?

Take a moment to do a short exercise. What do you like about yourself? Look at yourself from the viewpoint of someone else. What are your best qualities? What good things have you accomplished so far in your life? What good things can you still accomplish? Take a few moments to think and feel positively about yourself. Acknowledging the positive thoughts you have about yourself will have a lot to do with the way you will act.

Does your self-image include any of the traits of creativity, competence, talent, generosity, compassion or self-confidence? To the extent that you can feel these traits within you, you are in touch with your power, with the God within you. Some people call it being centered, being right with yourself or being at peace. Some of us have experienced this only a few times, some more often and some at higher levels than others. It can make a big difference in your life and it can be wonderful. This experience of empowerment can be enhanced and a consistent part of your daily life.

When we look closely at examples of great people, we see they all had a vision, an inner power, and they all believed in their own power. We have all used this power as well and most of us retain the memory of it. It shows up in such modest gestures as a friendly smile, as well as in great endeavors. But because we have stopped acknowledging our power, we rarely use it to its fullest, and it lies dormant within each of us, waiting to be freed.

RELATING AND SHARING

If everyone thought just like we do, we wouldn't need long conversations to let others know what we're thinking or how we're feeling. We would always be understood and we would be in agreement over just about everything. Imagine how boring that would be.

As much as we claim to want to communicate, most of us wouldn't want others to know everything we think and feel. Sometimes we are proud and happy with our differences and we feel that these differences are why others like or love us—because we are different from anyone else. Many times, however, we hope they won't discover the real us, our weaknesses and fears, because they may stop loving us.

Don: In my experience, both men and women harbor doubts, with their own variations. Yet we don't know exactly how similar our individual feelings are to the feelings of others.

Women are generally better than men at sharing their feelings. Just sharing them, however, doesn't always mean we will feel better or find a solution. We all have similar fears to cope with. Men have started to open up in these areas in the last few years, but it is still frightening and not okay to be open and vulnerable. Of the men I have talked to, most feel that they have to be strong, reliable and successful in order to be desirable to women. They must be comfortable with other men and feel they must have all the answers. It seems that people still admire men's strengths, but have little acceptance for our weaknesses. So to be open and show our doubts and weaknesses makes us vulnerable.

In the past, when a woman has encouraged me to open up, and when I have, they have said "that's enough," or it frightened them that I wasn't always the strong man they had counted on. It seemed like a trap in that if I didn't open up, I wouldn't meet their desires for intimacy, so I would lose; and if I did show my lack of strength in certain areas, it would frighten them away.

Our relationship with ourselves is mirrored in our relationships with others. When we protect ourselves and hide our vulnerabilities, we are hiding a part of ourselves from ourselves. The people around us provide a sounding board for who we are and how what we are doing affects them and ourselves. When we are as open as possible with others, without trying to manipulate them or allowing them to manipulate us, we are able to see ourselves most clearly. Sharing ourselves, experiencing emotional intimacy, provides the clearest view. When we see ourselves clearly, know who we really are, and what we stand for, and we can identify our aspirations and our dreams, we are touching our power—the spiritual core within each of us that empowers us to realize our highest selves.

Blaming others curtails our power.

For most of us, blaming and criticizing others for some of our problems, our dissatisfactions and frustrations is such an ingrained habit it is almost automatic. We revert back to this even when we try not to. And while there are certain circumstances where others have acted improperly, it is good to remember a basic tenet of human existence: everyone is doing the best they can, based on their past, their needs, their perceptions, their abilities and the depth of their wisdom. Just like we are doing the best we can. If we truly understand and believe this, we can neither blame others nor ourselves. The sooner we grasp this, the further along we will be in creating a full and powerful life for ourselves.

LANGUAGE VERSUS REALITY

We say we need to describe things succinctly so we don't have confusion and can understand each other. However, it seems sometimes that the more we attempt to define our respective positions, the more we get into trouble. In the areas of business, science, law and politics, we try to make our definitions tighter but instead of clarifying issues, some discussions become more difficult.

We are able to produce vast quantities of words of descriptions, brochures, legislation and litigation. But, many times aren't we missing the point? We define a flower by describing its component parts—its petals, sepals, stamen and pollen, but we tend to leave out the qualities of its fragrance and color, the gracefulness of its shape, and the glow it brings, when present in numbers, to an ordinary field.

A part of exercising self-empowerment is remembering that defined things are limited things, and that the closer we can get to our subjective impressions of life, the closer we are to the truth of life.

*The more we truly understand life
the less we can define it.*

We Can Make a Difference in the World

We are surrounded by a world that seems to have lost much of its spiritual, moral and ethical foundations. To use the vernacular, it has become a cover-your-ass society where protecting one's self—looking out for Number 1—has become the norm. We see it, we know it, but we do little. Why? Probably because we are so busy just surviving, just making it, and because the problems seem so overwhelming and unsolvable.

The problems are not overwhelming and they are solvable. Crime has decreased in areas where Neighborhood Watch volunteer groups are operating. Mothers Against Drunk Driving (MADD), through its courageous campaign, has helped to significantly reduce alcohol-related driving fatalities. These organizations are made up of self-empowered people who are no longer content to sit back and not get involved.

We have seen across the country an adopt-a-highway program, where different people or organizations have taken responsibility for removing trash from highways. We could carry this idea further and have an adopt-a-park, adopt-a-street or adopt-a-school program. We can reclaim these areas around us and help them serve the purpose for which they were intended.

If a group of concerned people were active at a park or on a street, the drug pushers and undesirables would feel less comfortable using these areas for tearing society apart. We can reclaim these places without confrontation. There are many people with free time and resources who can put their talents to use in schools. There are many more areas where we can act.

As we begin to retrieve our power, which also means increasing our ability to do things that need doing, our truest self whispers to us that it must be used—for the good of all—that unused power is no power at all.

Our power tells us that we must assume responsibility for the condition of our world—that we must be heard.

Self-Empowerment gives us the confidence that we will be heard, that we will make a difference.

This chapter has presented some ways in which we can regain our personal power. The next chapter describes a number of ways in which we can use our power to improve our world. So let's go.

7

A Vision of the World We Want

A GROUNDSWELL OF CHANGE

When one part of our body is sick we don't ignore it—we understand that sickness in one area can affect the entire body. Similarly, the inner city gangs, the urban homeless, the addicts, the career criminals and the lack of help or hope can no longer be thought of as simply other people's problems. They are going to get us all if we don't deal with them.

> *Our country does have enough for all,
> but our resources aren't getting
> to the people and the places
> where they are needed.*

If we approach our national and local problems with the same creativity, urgency and resources we bring to winning a foreign war we can and will solve our problems. We need to open up our thinking and open up the restrictions and limits we have put on ourselves.

Where are we stuck? What are our resources? What are our limits, and are they real or merely concocted? What are our true limits? Are we going to wait until there are gangs, violence and homelessness in all of our cities and towns? Are we going to wait until our welfare costs have overwhelmed us as has happened in New York City or wait until our government is totally ineffective? We are still the richest country in the world and we spend more money on social problems than any other country in the world—but it isn't working. How much longer can we wait for effective action?

On a larger scale, our world is getting smaller and smaller. Our systems of trade, our communication systems and the speed of modern travel all serve to bring disparate cultures together for enrichment and, also, conflict. The single, vast, interconnected international system which is emerging, like any other increasingly complex system, is becoming more fragile and more in need of care and balance. While the needs of the world increase exponentially, our solutions to world problems lag more and more behind. Populations are soaring unhindered and more people are starving in spite of increased aid programs; more areas of the earth are being denuded and robbed of their resources by avaricious business practices and by ignorant and weak governments. We are running out of time. None of us will have power or even a modestly successful life if the world becomes sicker and falters.

After World War II, most of the European continent was destroyed and unable to help itself. Through the massive (and very expensive) effort of the Marshall Plan, the United States helped rebuild much of postwar Europe. As a nation, we took great pride in this endeavor, and rightly so. By giving the Europeans the means to help themselves, we enhanced their self-esteem and their ability to improve on their own. The result, half a century later, is an economically healthy, dynamic region which is one of the great contributors to the modern world.

When nations, communities, and individuals work together to enhance each other's power, the possibilities for good are limitless. If a leader of a country uses his energy, his military or the resources of his people to control or suppress those under his rule or to fight others, he is wasting power. This takes tremendous energy away from all who are involved and leaves everyone worse off than if people were empowered and working together. If we have to watch others to make sure they're not a threat, then we are expending energy being defensive and making sure we are protected ourselves. If both take the same stance, it steals energy from each and neither will be able to live empowered, creative, fulfilled lives.

When defensiveness is taken to an extreme, the world sees leaders such as Sadam Hussein of Iraq. As a child Sadam was beaten and threatened. His only role model taught him that power was acquired through the ability to control. This was achieved by beating other people and causing them to operate out of fear in order to keep them in line. This, of course, leads to the development of paranoia. In this environment, Sadam Hussein felt he had to remove all the other leaders through assassinating them. He could only remain powerful if he took away their power, encouraged their weaknesses and didn't allow people in his country any feelings of personal power. This has left a country which is very rich in oil and other resources in a fearful, unadvanced, uneducated state where its people have no freedom and no power of their own.

Like that of all tyrants, Sadam's power is counterfeit and he must live in a constantly defensive mode, forever suspicious, unsure and wondering how long it will last. Anytime we see this kind of counterfeit power in the world we see oppression, we see lack of economic growth, we see things not working for the benefit of all. To the extent that we support the arming, the aggression and the violent philosophies of foreign governments, sometimes on both sides, we are supporting the waste of power and the promotion of weakness.

COMMUNITIES THAT WORK

The true definition of community is a group of people whose lives are deeply interconnected and who care about each other. Unfortunately, fewer and fewer areas in the United States have any sense of community. This loss gives rise to depersonalization—living among and interacting with people whom we don't know and don't care about.

Community is about people cooperating with people.
It is a concept that reaches beyond streets, neighborhoods, cities or even national borders.

We get feedback from other people's reactions to us that help us know who we are. No one can live in total isolation from people. Most of us identify community as our immediate family, our extended family, or our ethnic family. Many are looking into their roots or ethnic background to get insight into where their values came from.

To the extent that we are self-empowered—with love, mutual respect and integrity—we'll have a good relationship with others both within and outside of our own communities.

All communities, whether on a local or national scale, have rules. We make rules and then have representatives make laws for our benefit. For large communities, the laws become so complicated that we need a judicial system to interpret them for us. Then we have police enforce the rules, and armies to maintain them between national communities.

Communities function as long as the individuals have more incentives to support them instead of going against them. When community interests provide freedom, benefits and fairness to the people, they are motivated within themselves to support their interests and the stability and health of the community. When they don't, we have more police, checking, enforcing, taking and people trying to get away with more and get more than they give.

In chapter 2 we commented on types of communities that don't work. Here, we are introduced to some communities that do work, and one of the best examples as we mentioned in chapter 3, is the Delancey Street Foundation of San Francisco.

Delancey Street, a residence program for mostly ex-convicts is almost entirely self-supporting. It trains each member in four different trades and operates profit-making businesses which utilize their skills.

Robert Rocha is an example of one individual's experience with Delancey Street. He had no father and his mother had been in and out of prison all during his childhood. Robert had been in foster homes since he was eight years old. In his teens he carried a gun, sold drugs and stole whatever he could lay his hands on. Finally, he was arrested and convicted of twenty-seven armed robberies. Robert spent two years in San Quentin. After he was released, in 1987, he was convicted again for selling heroin to an undercover cop.

Like other newcomers to Delancey Street, Robert started out filled with bitterness. He didn't give a damn about anyone else and tried to keep away from all the other residents. Gradually, he made a few friends. One day, after he had been in the program for about eight months, one of his friends decided to drop out and go back to the street. Before he realized what he was doing, Robert found himself pleading with the other man to stay, not to give up this chance to get right. "Don't ruin it, man. Hang in! Don't go back to that life!"

Before that day, Robert had never pleaded with any-one for anything. Now he suddenly found that he cared—he actually cared for someone. When he realized that, he burst out crying and years of bitterness and despair drained out of him.

Today, four years after going on parole, Robert is twenty-six and has learned eight construction trades. He is taking college level courses in criminology and he helps other ex-cons earn their high school diplomas. He has become a stable, productive, eminently decent member of society, and at Delancey Street he is not an exception.

Mimi Silbert came from an immigrant neighborhood in Boston, where her father ran the corner drugstore. "Delancey Street functions in the way my own family did," she says.

Delancey Street has strict rules - no alcohol, drugs, threats or violence, to name a few. In order to be accepted for residency, newcomers must ask to be admitted—in writing—and must promise to remain for at least two years. Eighty percent of the residents keep that promise. Graduates include successful lawyers, businessmen, technicians and construction workers.

At the heart of this unique "extended family" is the spirit and unswerving resolve of Dr. Mimi Silbert, 49, a criminologist. Since 1972, she has dedicated her life to keeping Delancey Street open and growing. An elfin woman weighing less than 100 pounds, she stands toe-to-toe with the meanest, toughest ex-felons until the shouting turns into laughter, tears and hard work. Here deep wounds have an opportunity to gradually heal.

"You want to quit?" she challenged Robert Rocha and other Delancey Street residents while they were building their new San Francisco complex on the waterfront. "Well," Silbert told them, "that's what you've always done— given up every time it has gotten difficult! I know you're hammering away and thinking that this isn't worth it but you're hammering away on your own lives.

"You're building your own foundation. If you make a mistake with that wall, tear it down and rebuild it! That's what we're doing at Delancey Street, for ourselves—tearing down bad things and making good things to replace 'em. And if you're too guilty and angry and hopeless to fight for yourself, then do it for the next guy. Because he's counting on you. Meanwhile, you're learning new skills. You're getting something that nobody can take away from you. You're building your lives."

There are 500 current residents in the San Francisco complex which opened in 1990. About 500 others are going through this same rigorous program in Brewster, N.Y; in

Greensboro, N.C.; and in San Juan Pueblo, N.M. With neither funding nor a permanent staff other than Silbert herself, Delancey Street is almost entirely self-supporting. Its business enterprises, run by residents, net $3 million a year.

"We're trying to prove that the 'losers' in our society can, in fact, be helped," Silbert says, "and also that they, in turn, can help. Essentially they make up an underclass. A third of our population was homeless. The average resident is four or five generations into poverty and two or three generations into prison. They've been hard-core dope fiends. They've had horrible violence done to them and they've been violent."

Today the Delancey Street program is being studied by groups all over the United States, in hopes of duplicating this successful community on a larger scale.

Communities, with the right ingredients, can and do work. They empower the people within them and they empower themselves.

True power is people helping people live to their highest potential.

In Bali, we experienced communities that were really working. No one was starving or homeless. We have equal abundance and a hundred times their wealth yet some of America's children are going to bed hungry and are wandering the streets, homeless.

In Bali, farmers work twelve hours a day, six days a week with crude implements and water buffalo. They work hard, yet they share what they have so no one starves. Their customs are steeped in tradition and ritual. They celebrate life with festivals, dancing, music, art and they make offerings to God daily. Their sense of community and belonging is natural to their culture. Everyone belongs.

We experienced cooperation even in their driving habits. When a person wanted to pass or go ahead of another it was done in a friendly and courteous way by both parties. They live in harmony and respect each other, as well as the land that feeds them.

There are many different kinds of effective communities. One of them is Alcoholics Anonymous, a well known spiritual community of the heart. There are hundreds of meetings daily all around the world, attended by millions of alcoholics who are staying sober one day at a time by practicing the 12 Steps of this program. It is a fellowship of people who are mutually empowered by sharing their common experience, strength and hope, and who stay sober with the help of a Higher Power.

M. Scott Peck, in his book, *The Different Drum—Community-Making and Peace* has looked into communities and the community-making process. He gives examples of communities that work and gives seminars where you can experience community building in a few days.

As we live in integrity, with respect for others, we empower our communities. As we empower our communities, they empower us and we are better for living in them. The rewards are tremendous.

Many of us have gotten away from our communities. We move around the country, following job opportunities; we meet and marry someone from another state; or we may find ourselves suddenly transferred from one facility of a company to another in a different location. After many years of transiency, we begin to long for closer community ties. We find that we want to get back into community relationships and to bond with others like ourselves. Everything from 12-Step programs to men's groups are becoming popular to help us support each other and to learn and feel how other people deal with situations similar to our own. There are parent's support groups, children's support groups, support groups for cancer, AIDS and other diseases. There are also Boy Scouts, church, and social and service groups.

When two or more persons are gathered together in common cause, more power can be generated. We see great things being accomplished every day in our society by very small groups. In the United States, a small, vocal minority can exert tremendous power and influence for their cause.

We can choose to be part of a community of special interests or we can be in a diverse community of people who simply enjoy being together. A common factor of community, whatever its ultimate purpose, is the support of each other's integrity, energy and interests; and helping each member understand and accomplish their purpose in life. The key here is that people are together to build each other up, not to tear each other down. They are there to be truthful and honest, not brag and compete. They are there to aid and add insight, not ridicule and demean.

These groups are available to all of us, and can be formed by us individually. Get a group together of people who want to improve their lives, start their own business, take an interest in improving the environment, improve the community, help with employment or gangs or drugs. The empowerment of this common interest, with very simple guidelines, can produce tremendous results. Based on our own experience with various groups, some guidelines you may want to consider for your own group are as follows:

- Have a simple, understandable format with positive goals and rules.

- Meet regularly for short periods of time.

- Share the leadership and running of the meeting with everyone having an equal say.

- Don't discuss any member's personal life, situation or activities unless that person asks for feedback.

- Insist on honesty and integrity—no ego plays or boasting.

- Encourage and support people in their aspirations and being all that they can be.

- Maintain confidentiality among the participants.

- Make sure the group is a listening group. There are too many groups where people think only of what they are going to say next, rather than listening and caring about what is being said by other people.

There are areas in our country where rehabilitation programs and sharing groups are working very effectively, and they can be duplicated. We need to find new approaches to our many problems, and one of the best ways to do this is to combine and multiply our creativity, our energy and our resources.

RECLAIMING OUR HEROES

Remember, from Chapter 3, the story of the San Francisco cabby who pinned a mugger against a wall with his cab and was then sued by the convicted mugger for "excessive use of force?" We need a new law which reaffirms that a charge of using excessive force, while trying to stop or apprehend someone who is committing a violent crime, can only be brought against an individual if that individual has used force maliciously or with a deliberate attempt to excessively injure rather than to merely apprehend the criminal. Since the states have jurisdiction over these laws as part of their police powers, under the constitution, we need to contact our state representatives, our state attorney general and our state bar association and let them know we want this change in the law. We should demand that they act to enable courageous citizens to do their moral duty without fear of legal reprisal.

Let's bring acts of unselfish
courage and heroism
into the mainstream of our society.

A step in the right direction would be to once again focus attention on individuals who can be an inspiration to ourselves and to our children. Perhaps it would be of benefit for each of us to pause during our busy schedule, and make a short list of our contemporary heroes.

Stretch your wings and be heroic.

If you have children, discuss the idea of heroes with them. Find out who their heroes are and tell them about yours. It's time we all regained some of our power and our right to help determine who our heroes will be.

PEOPLE AND THE PRIVATE SECTOR

People have gotten into the habit of bad-mouthing business, as though there is something inherently wrong with doing something worthwhile, succeeding at it and making a profit from our labors. Every once in awhile it's good to stop and remember that the private sector is what makes everything else possible. There wouldn't be government, social services and help for the needy without businesses creating wealth. The relatively high standard of living that we have enjoyed has come from business, and the health of our country is directly related to the health of the private sector. Yes, we have to take care of human rights and our environment, but capitalism and profit are not dirty words. We, as a nation, because of our business freedom, have given more to others than any other country in the world. It is a record of which we can proud.

We have also been shortsighted. We have taken the attitude that if we care for the majority of people, the minority will be okay as well. Unfortunately, this is not the case. As we've said earlier our country has enough food and can provide enough shelter and health care for everyone without there having to be any extra burden on anyone. We have the economic resources to do this. It is a matter of organizing our resources properly. We have enough worthwhile projects to employ everyone, even those people who are traditionally considered unemployable. We are not doing this. With the help of companies, some communities have made it possible for everyone who wants to work to be able to do so. Being able to work is very important for an individual's self-esteem and the health of our communities and country as a whole.

Any individual should be able to supply his family's basic needs without welfare.

Anyone not working to their capacity, who wants to, is wasting their ability, and our country is under-utilizing that person as a resource. Many people are idle even though they would rather not be. If we could put more of this idle time to work it would be better for these individuals and we would receive tremendous benefit from using these human resources.

It's easy to say that helping individuals and communities is the job of the government. That's partially true, but we then get to the dilemma of too much government, which currently means inefficiency and implementation handled too far away from the situation it is intended to help. Thus we have an ineffective, non-working, and much-resented program. An alternative to government handling local and regional projects is for business to develop solutions to meet these needs with the participation of their employees.

Government programs can also be contracted to private companies effectively.

The bottom line of a company's profits can be positively affected by including social services as a part of their benefits package. Some companies have decided to do this on their own; others have been forced into offering social programs. Health care, parking, sick leave, company and employee security, safety, child care, recreation, addiction programs and education for employees and dependents are among a few of the worthwhile programs that have helped the image of companies (and actually increased profits as well).

By creative thinking we can come up with good business solutions to many social problems. For example, Japanese companies have had the policy of not laying people off; they have been forced to devise ways to use these available workers effectively. Rather than a burden, this social obligation has caused companies to train workers in multiple skills. In construction, field superintendents get involved in estimating and bidding when work is slow. Who better knows these costs than someone who works with them directly.

It has merit for people to switch from production to improving production techniques, quality assurance or even sales when business is slow. Employees become more valuable to themselves and their companies; their varied abilities are used, not lost. The results have been more productive, satisfied workers and high quality products. So attending to human values in the work force is not incompatible with efficiency and profit—on the contrary, in the long run it is a boost to efficiency and profit.

Let's look at the problems of our unemployed in this light. These people are being fed and housed anyway; let's put them to work for their own benefit and the benefit of the country. Our business leaders need to act now, instead of waiting for the government to do it (less efficiently).

We need to get back our can-do attitude.

Our goal should be to give everyone an opportunity to make a positive contribution. Education and learning is a key to accomplishing this.

EDUCATION—LEARNING?

Our students are not getting as good an education as possible or being empowered through education. We need to encourage them to appreciate their worth, be capable of earning a living and learn to love learning and knowledge. We have lost sight of the purpose of education. We can change this!

Concepts Vital to Empowered Learning:

• Learn about learning and the excitement of learning as a life-long experience versus grading and evaluating their work.

• Learn about who and what we are.

• Learn respect for ourselves, others, our social systems and environment.

• Learn self-confidence, self-esteem and self-actualization.

• Learn economics, how to handle money, save, prepare for emergencies, medical and retirement.

• Learn intuitive thinking in addition to linear thinking.

• Learn to think, reason, solve problems, think for self and be a free thinker, instead of using predominately rote memory.

• Learn to question values, laws and customs so they can either confirm their value or the need for change.

• Learn about leadership, following and cooperation.

• Learn how government really operates, and how people can bring about changes through legitimate, legal means, instead of lawbreaking or civil disobedience.

• Learn to earn a living and use attributes and gifts.

• Learn about family and community; cooperation and co-creation.

• Learn value systems, the importance of quality success and how to succeed in life.

• Learn about body, mind and most of all our spirituality and connectedness to the universe.

•Learn about stress and how to cope with it.

• Learn to contemplate the meaning of life.

The "three R's" (reading, writing, arithmetic) are important as well as science, art, music, history, etc., and the appreciation of learning to enhance a person's entire life. We need to measure the results of our education system. Measuring one student against another, (not being the best in sports or other subjects) instead of himself or what needs to be learned can actually de-motivate them. It causes lots of students to only strive for ratings or grades (external motivation) rather than doing their best.

Learning for enjoyment, satisfaction and the benefits of knowledge in our lives should be our true goal. Cheating will be less likely when the learning is for the individual's benefit and by internal motivation. Learning can be a wonderful enriching experience for our entire lives. It helps keep us young open and adaptable. We can make it fun!

The Japanese require and provide a far better education for their young people than we do. They go to school approximately fifty more days a year than our students. Their education is geared more towards what they expect to do in their working lifetime. Our country doesn't really get students involved in what they expect to do until they are well into high school and college—and sometimes never. We educate a lot of people to get degrees, and the result is that many of them are not geared to earn an income or productively benefit themselves or our country. We need to fundamentally change our educational system to allow students to be better prepared for the jobs and entrepreneurial businesses that will be needed.

BUSINESS OPERATIONS AND ETHICS

Like individual people, companies have personalities and identities—they each have a unique spirit and feeling about them. We all know companies that we feel good about and trust, and we also are aware of companies we don't trust at all. The overall feeling and ethics of a company permeate an organization with or without formal manuals and policies. Sometimes the actual, working ethics of a company are even opposite the official or stated policy. Not being in integrity by having the stated polices and values of the company conflict with the actual working values of the company is very disempowering.

As an example, some companies have a stated warranty or return program but when someone tries to get satisfaction, they are harassed and the paperwork or procedure is extremely difficult. We recently bought a laser printer that didn't work. After a week of phoning and getting busy signals and "we are busy" recordings, we had no choice but to return the item. This cost the company far more than a policy that is consistant and works. Companies have gone out of business, had high employee turnover and low employee and customer loyalty because of these inconsistencies.

Almost everyone has worked in a business or other organization where the rules were known but everyone ignored them. This inconsistency between stated and actual values is a box that severely limits companies. Most people want to, and will do, a good job if they are appreciated and allowed to participate in the factors that affect their jobs. When they are not given these opportunities, they become de-motivated. This drains more productivity and positive energy out of a company than any other factor. People will, either subconsciously or openly, work against their own company if they don't understand, believe in and participate in its policies.

Don: I have had many experiences of hearing, "This is our policy," or "We can't do this" and then had fellow employees explain how I could get around the particular policy or limit. Even a boss can tell you how to do it but qualifies it with "Don't tell anyone I told you."

Sometimes I was even told to get the needed part or service from a competitor rather than fight the restrictions of my own employer. Other times, it has been suggested to me that I do a job in such a way that it deliberately cost the company or client more money.

Many companies are unaware of the harm they are doing to themselves. Many just accept their behavior as the norm and don't realize the tremendous costs they incur. Inconsistency, lack of integrity, false limits and rules, and lack of vision are very costly both to companies and to the individuals in them. Changing these de-motivators can give fantastic improvement to all areas of business.

*W*e need to create a minimal standard of business ethics in the United States.

For many managers it has become the norm to adopt the attitude, "What is the most we can get and the least we can give?" Another, cruder way of saying this is that we take whatever we can get away with and let others look out for their own interests. On the surface, this is the best way to maximize profit in a business, at least in the short run. But in the long run it always backfires.

We need a national ethic that encourages businesses to adopt policies which will benefit all others with whom they are involved—policies of mutual benefit. If this isn't done, employees will follow the ethical lead of their management and look out only for themselves. Customers are also affected by the lack of management ethics because the entire company will be influenced by management's lead, and customers sense it.

Many companies miss this subtle idea in dealing with employees and with the public. When we look out for ourselves at the expense of others there is something of value that is lost. Employees are less motivated, there is incentive to "get even" or "get their turn next time." Anytime you aren't extra-vigilant, someone will take advantage of you. Ethics aside, this wastes a lot of energy and money.

So when we talk about revitalizing our industries, let's include revitalizing our business ethics to reflect the highest standards. If we do this, it will help to stop the continuing decline of business in America. The only way to maintain an efficient, profit-making, human-oriented business climate in our country over the long run is by having all of our power working for us. This means creating an environment of support for employees, products, other assets, customers, the community and our world. Anytime one or more of these areas become disempowered, it affects us all.

The private sector has traditionally been one of the leaders in making progress and finding new solutions for society. The way we operate our businesses will go a long way toward determining the kind of country we are going to be living in.

Adversarial Law

There are many types of businesses that conduct themselves regularly in an adversarial way. Two lawyers representing their respective clients oftentimes become the worst examples of failing to work agreements out to the benefits of both parties. In legal battles we often lose perspective in our quest for victory. It then becomes more important who has the best lawyer, who is the shrewdest or how one can get the advantage or put the other at a disadvantage.

This "I win/you lose" model leaves a hollow victory because in an increasing number of cases, lawyers take a large percentage of the settlement. This method has made heroes out of people who often lack compassion, care or consideration for what effect this has in the long run on those concerned. High fee percentages and promoting adversarial actions may be legal, but they were not the intent when our laws were set up.

There are many examples of adversarial relations where both sides lose. Many contracts are entered into from this basis rather than from a win-win attitude. The auto industry and its unions have been taught a humbling lesson by the Japanese and their cooperative management style. There are many American company/union cases where each side has destroyed the other. The hard feelings and de-motivation that remain can weaken or destroy the ones we work with and count on, and can cause irreparable long-term damage.

Any time people do as little as they can get away with (and this is written into some union contracts), everyone is losing. This is power robbing, which gives no one security and produces the opposite results of what we want. We don't need more lawyers fighting more adversary battles by using ambiguous or vague rules.

When legal issues are involved it is helpful to understand the nature of the adversarial system. The responsibility of your lawyer is to protect your rights, not necessarily to resolve conflicts through non-legal means. If he or she doesn't protect your rights, your lawyer may be liable. Therefore, if a lawsuit occurs, your lawyer will try to make sure that every word, every phrase and every detail is aired in court.

This is what our adversarial system demands. The law firm, in order to be certain that your rights are legally protected and that it can't be held liable for mistakes or poor representation, may carry the case to the "nth" degree, with cost as a secondary priority. Of course, in doing this, the law firm will make money. In fact, the monetary gains of the law firm, on the one hand, and protecting your rights, on the other, have become so intertwined that it is difficult to separate them. The most important thing to understand from this is that a lawyer's method of protecting your rights is sometimes not in your best interest. The following story illustrates this clearly.

I recall the case of Winnie Myers and her two sons. Winnie's husband had died two years earlier. For years, he had talked to his advisers alone and had never included other family members in these discussions. After he died, the older son stepped in to try to manage the family company. In doing so, he incurred a debt of nine hundred thousand dollars and he was having trouble repaying it. After being served with a notice of default on the loan, Winnie went to her attorney, a very bright, competent man, and asked, "What can we do about the debt?"

"It's going to court," he said. "You signed a continuing guarantee and the bank has filed suit to collect on it. You don't have a choice."

From the legal viewpoint, her lawyer was right. And the suit was justified from the viewpoint of the lawyer representing the bank. But is it in the best interest of the family to settle the lawsuit out of court or not?

For some lawyers, their sincere perception is that the courtroom is the fairest and easiest way to resolve conflict, and courtrooms are where they can practice their art and earn their livelihood. But my experience tells me that the very last thing you want to do is go to court. My experience tells me that what is needed is for all the parties to sit down together and negotiate.

When I became involved, I was able to get the family and the bank officers to sit down together. When all the facts were on the table, it became apparent that Winnie's company had been a good customer of the bank for a long time and that the company was basically sound. These were factors that hadn't been obvious from the legal documents. In just forty-five minutes, we were able to agree to dismiss the lawsuit and to negotiate payments in such a way that the family business could continue and the bank would feel secure about their loan. It was a win-win solution.[1]

We need to return "justice" to our legal system, and while we are doing it, let's see if we can't return common sense to it as well.

Ethics In Government

For a long time, serving in government was considered an honor which carried with it certain obligations. Among them were the obligations to serve the people selflessly, fairly and with integrity. But over the past decades, the ethical standards of behavior for political office have gradually deteriorated, and it will be a long road back to the high ethical standards which once were the hallmark of American politics.

Once, we assumed that anyone we elected would act honorably; now we no longer know. One beginning step can be to require all of our elected officials, especially those in higher offices, to take a simple pledge, along these lines:

I will never knowingly lie to the American people. When it is clearly in the best interests of this nation to withhold certain information from the public, I will do so only to the minimum extent necessary and only for

the minimum time period necessary. I will never knowingly withhold information or lie to the American
people in order to avoid embarrassment to myself, my
staff, my party or my cause.

I promise never to knowingly pursue illegal means
or to influence or suggest or condone that my staff
pursue illegal means to further a cause, even though I
deem it to be just and right.

I agree not to dishonor the political process by
participating in personal attacks on political opponents,
nor will I allow any member of my staff, or others
whose actions I am able to influence to do so.

Where there is a conflict between my personal
goals and the good of the country, I will do my best to
follow the course which is best for the country.

So simple. So obvious. And yet what a difference it
could make. If you want to take a step toward prodding
the government to be more accountable and honest, start
by showing this pledge to your congressman and senators,
and to your state legislators; show it to reporters and radio
and TV personalities. Show it to everyone you know, and
ask them to pass it on.

RUNNING GOVERNMENT AS A BUSINESS

The government gets a lot of static these days on the
way it conducts its business. Some of this even comes from
workers within government agencies who are frustrated
by not being able to implement improvements, enable
work efficiencies or help solve many of the problems of
which they are a part. Being in an inefficient organization

where our efforts aren't appreciated or used effectively is demoralizing and takes away our power.

Over the years, departments and levels of the government have each established their own "turf." They are separate from each other and they cooperate with other departments to the minimum extent possible. Each department often has its own procedures, forms and schedules which are unnecessarily duplicated in other departments. Unofficially, some departments are called power centers, but the power the managers of these departments have is the ability to hold up the actions of others.

It is time to start running government like a business.

This means that managers and workers in government have to become aware of the competition. Examples of competition are: how United Parcel Service and Federal Express are giving the Post Office fits; how businesses move from one community or state to another because of governmental regulations, paperwork or taxes; we even lose some businesses to other countries because of government costs. Governments must use all of their resources effectively or they are wasting our money. They have to treat the public like valued customers. They have to be open to change, and keep in mind the purpose of their particular department or agency.

All too often, civil servants come to regard procedures as the most important part of their mission and the correct use of vast amounts of paperwork has taken the place of the original purpose—to provide services and solve problems. This results in priorities being turned upside-down. For example, needy welfare recipients are frequently denied payments because the paperwork they submit is incorrect, even though they are otherwise eligible.

Contrast this with a part of the private sector...the banking industry, for example. Banks compete vigorously with each other for our business. If you went into your bank to make a withdrawal from your account and you filled in one line of the form incorrectly, what would happen? The teller would either make the needed correction immediately or help you to do it. Can you imagine how long your bank would stay in business if they turned you away because you had made an error on a form?

The incentive that a business has to become efficient is that if they don't, a competitor will and they'll be out-of-business. We read every day about private industries reorganizing and making difficult changes to keep up with the times. There is little incentive in government organizations or agencies to become efficient. When taxes are cut, or when they are put in some other squeeze, government agencies often do not become more efficient—they simply cut back their services without fundamentally changing anything. It's almost a "we'll show you" or not admitting that they can cut back or streamline their operation.

Similarly, our legislators have no incentive to curtail their awarding of unnecessary projects to their own districts. On the contrary, they have an incentive to continue doing it so that they win the political and financial support of special interest groups. We need to turn this around and adopt a system where legislators are rewarded for their collective efficiency.

We need our government to become as effective in doing business as private enterprise. Without an incentive system, government will be hard to change. We need to establish competition between government agencies for raising standards of efficiency. We need to develop the option of subcontracting as many services as possible so that we can at least compare the efficiency of a government service to that of a business doing the same thing. It might even be worthwhile to subcontract some of the services of our Congress—at least the threat might scare them enough to perform the ways in which we expect. Does it serve us for them to spend a great deal of their time campaigning and raising money to be re-elected instead of what they are paid to do?

> *Business executives are rewarded*
> *based on their performance,*
> *why not legislators?*

We need to encourage our elected officials and government administrators to pay more attention to the end purpose of their departments. Providing incentives for government workers to suggest ways in which overlapping services can be eliminated and the task done more efficiently would be beneficial. As it now works, the system rewards supervisors for having more employees under them. This trend needs to be reversed to reward supervisors for getting their job done with fewer people and more efficiency.

*We must insist on
clearer accountability
for the ways in which
our tax money is spent.*

Operating a business demands that we know the costs of overhead as compared to costs for actually producing a product or service. For example, an employee lounge, maintaining a parking lot and administrative costs are part of overhead. If the ratio of overhead costs to the actual costs of producing the product become too high, the business will not be able to compete and will probably fail. So most businesses work hard to reduce their overhead costs. We even judge nonprofit, charitable organizations by how much money they use for administration versus how much money actually goes into the programs. Since these figures are published, we can tell which charities are operating efficiently and which are wasting much of their money.

But we have no similar way to evaluate government.

*We need to ask:
What percentage of a government
budget is being used for its programs
and what percentage is going to
paperwork, staff and other less
essentials?*

The following shows how workers and management have come together in common purpose, in industry and in government, to create greater efficiencies. There are many stories like these, we need many more.

Facing unprecedented competition, often from overseas, more employers are abandoning management practices that have often let alienation replace motivation in the workplace. They are cracking down on excessive absenteeism, high defect rates and idleness on the job by picking, training and rewarding subordinates differently. And in many industries, aided by worried union leaders, management is getting results. A key reason is a change in management practices.

Among other approaches, more corporations are using self-managed teams to rejuvenate the work ethic. Typically, a team replaces the boss by controlling everything from schedules to hiring and, sometimes, firing. This "empowerment" trend, which emerged during the 1980's at major manufacturers such as Digital Equipment Corp. and Corning Inc., now is moving from the factory into the white-collar service sector, including banks and mutual funds.

About one in five US. employers operates self-managed teams today, up from one in 20 a decade ago.

THE TEAM APPROACH

By the mid-1980's, Chrysler Corp. was ready to shut its oldest plant, a dingy and rundown components facility in rural New Castle, Ind., that was beset by heavy absenteeism and worker alienation.

"If they wanted us to run [make] five parts, we would

run two" just for spite, recollects John Pennington, a 48-year-old machine-setup man. "I missed work when I wanted to miss work, at times staying home drunk," he says. When a machine breakdown halted production, the $17.26-an-hour employee adds, "We'd drink coffee and just wait for the problem to get corrected," by managers.

In 1986, the United Auto Workers Union and Chrysler decided to attempt to save New Castle by creating teams, aided by consultants Kepner-Tregoe Inc. Workers were renamed "technicians" and line supervisors—some of whom left over the power loss—became "team advisers." Time clocks disappeared.

The plant's 77 teams now assign tasks, confront sluggish performers, order repairs, talk to customers and even alter work hours after consulting a labor-management steering committee. Extra training earns workers extra pay. When New Castle resumes hiring for the first time since 1977, possibly next year, teams will pick candidates.

"Employees have sort of taken ownership of this plant," says Ed Zachary, UAW Local 371 President. Absenteeism has plummeted to 2.9% from 7%. Union grievances tumbled to 33 in 1991; they used to exceed 1,000 a year. The number of defects per million parts made has fallen to 20 from 300 three years ago. And production costs keep shrinking.

No More Excuses

When Claire E. Freeman took over the Cuyahoga Metropolitan Housing Authority in June 1990, loafing was practically a way of life for the 600 maintenance workers at Cleveland's troubled public-housing agency.

As a result, buildings housing 17,000 families were covered with litter and graffiti. Tenants complained bitterly about waiting up to six months for maintenance employees to fix their leaky faucets and broken windows. Some tenants also said that they often noticed crews sitting under trees doing nothing.

Kevin Fagan, a 32-year old maintenance man at Cedar Extension Estate, says he remained idle for several hours at times because tools were broken or he couldn't find parts. But "quite a few" of his colleagues loafed because they lacked adequate supervision, Mr. Fagan adds.

Making matters worse, union rules forced the housing authority to assign overtime based on seniority. Employees won the lucrative extra duty "no matter if you did nothing the whole day, because you were the senior man," says Ronald T. Thorpe, Cedar Extension maintenance superintendent. So Ms. Freeman increased direct supervision. Cuyahoga also spent more than $100,000 to equip workshops and to provide every maintenance worker with tool sets. It built a mock apartment where employees learn to fix a toilet, do carpentry and mend wiring.

With the union's approval, Cuyahoga no longer promotes largely on seniority. "We realized the problem," says Cheryl DeLauer, the local's business agent. "Just because I am more senior doesn't mean I can necessarily handle the job." "We eliminated every excuse for idleness," Mr. Thorpe says. "Maintenance workers now are cleaning up," he boasts. "They are shoveling snow...they are picking up the trash. They might be pruning the trees-but they aren't sitting under them anymore."

Well, most of them aren't. A fourth of Mr. Thorpe's 24-person maintenance crew still "aren't giving us eight hours' work for eight hours pay," he says. "But it's hard to fire civil-service employees," he frets. [2]

These examples show how ideas like these can be implemented to make things better for both the public and the people working within the government.

In addition to lack of efficiency, another problem with government is that it insulates itself from its own actions. Our representatives have a unique style of taking credit when the outcomes are good, or jaw-boning about what they are going to do for us, but then their actions are contrary to what they say they are doing. If there are going to be bad results, it's not uncommon for a representative, who is constantly seeking public approval and votes, to assign a task force or study groups. He assigns other people down the line who are insulated from him, so he can say that the situation is so far removed from him that he can't control it.

Our government needs to be changed so it isn't insulated from us and indifferent to our needs.

We feel frustrated over our inability to control the IRS, the military, the defense department, sometimes the post office and many other bureaucratic agencies with which we interface. Government needs to follow the lead of successful private enterprises. Companies, from time to time, go in, from top to bottom and re-analyze what their purpose is, how they make their money, how they stay in business, how they compete and what services they should offer. They consider how they might revamp the organization to make themselves more effective towards reaching their goals, use and appreciate their people and their resources to their maximum and make sure they are accomplishing what they set out to do.

One of the biggest ways we've lost power in our country is by giving up control of our government and no longer having a government "by the people for the people." It has changed from the original intent over a long period of time in little ways. Every once in awhile we make some corrections and stop this loss of control. Now we are at a point where we have to take action in a big way. We have the ability to do this. It's important for us to get back involved with our government to get our control back. It's important for the people who work in our government to know that they are there to serve us in our democratic country.

*It's time for a major revision
in our government.*

CIVIL SERVICE

The civil service system was originally set up to operate much like private enterprise. This meant that workers were evaluated, rated, given promotions, pay raises and other normal employee benefits, as is done in private enterprise. Civil service employees could also be fired. However, by now it has become difficult if not impossible to fire an employee of the government. In some cases, one of the few ways a manager can get rid of an undesirable employee is to have him transferred to another department.

It is almost as difficult to reward an employee for doing extra fine work as it is to fire him. There are usually tests, smoke screens or other invalid standards to determine whether a person gets promoted or not, which are not always designed to rate effectiveness or ability to do the job. This can be changed by encouraging government to allow its employees to be creative, to have their resources used, to be appreciated and to enable them to become efficient in the work they are doing for us.

Most employees are good. The problem is that they are under-utilized, under-appreciated, under-listened-to and bogged down by rules, paperwork and bureaucracy in general. It is time that we tell our representatives, in no uncertain terms, that we want the civil service system managed by the standards and efficiencies of our best private enterprises.

THE DEFENSE INDUSTRY

One of the largest industries in our country is the defense industry, and the U.S. is the largest exporter of armaments in the world. In many cases, arms are sold to both sides of a conflict. So we are supplying destruction to both sides, rather than aiding and helping them to resolve their problems and live in peace.

One of the most consistent arguments for selling arms, and for our large defense industry in general, is that we need to help these people defend themselves, or provide a balance of power. But in truth we are weakening them. We are taking people away from productive activities and having them live either in fear or with attitudes of aggression. When people are trained to use arms, not trust their neighbor, be aggressive and destructive they don't have time, energy or emphasis on building homes, farms, industries or peace.

We are providing a balance of weakness
rather than a balance of power
by selling arms to opposing groups
around the world.

The two other big arguments in favor of a large arms industry are jobs and economy of scale. We all know about the jobs argument—that the defense department employs alot of people in many states and communities. The economy of scale argument claims that we need to have large overseas sales of our arms because they would cost too much for us to produce them in smaller quantities, just for our own use. But for how long can we justify the manufacture and distribution of super-lethal weapons, which are designed to efficiently kill and destroy, on the basis of jobs and profits? And is our only recourse to continue to produce weapons of mass destruction?

Our Defense Department was once called the War Department. We changed the name because it was no longer appropriate.

Changing the name of our
Defense Department to
Peace Department
will more accurately reflect our
intended purpose in the world.

This can better utilize our well- trained and dedicated people in the military. Their purpose is to promote peace anyway. It also sends a better, clearer message to the rest of the world. Defense can be part of the Peace Department which puts our organizations into alignment with our country's values.

We no longer have the Soviet Union as our big enemy (if they were ever the force we were told they were). Because some cuts in defense are inevitable, we talk about loss of jobs and loss of employment, but all of these potentially unemployed people, and then some, could be put into positive, productive efforts—farm machinery, fertilizers, new high-tech industries, manufacturing equipment, education, teaching, giving the people hope and faith—positive things in their lives rather than fear and destruction. Our country can produce and supply the food, medical care and all of our other needs. It's just a matter of reallocating our priorities and resources, and we are smart enough to do this if we change our thinking in that direction.

It is said by proponents of a large arms industry that if we don't export arms, other suppliers will, and we will lose jobs and lose our ability to influence the arms-buying countries for the better. But one has only to look at the evidence of how Japan increasingly influences other countries in the world without selling a single gun. Their influence is economic, based on their strong, non-defense industries. Japan's industries have created economy of scale not with tanks and missiles, but with TV's and cameras and cars.

The greatest influence of the future,
will be strong, efficient,
high-tech industries.

The sooner we can convert our arms-makers to peaceful production, the stronger and more influential we will become.

Think of the pride we can have if
we help peoples live better lives,
instead of helping to destroy them.

This is the kind of true power people enjoy. We aren't advocating not defending ourselves, because sometimes this is a necessary solution. As it is, however, our government defines "defense" as pretty much anything they want to do with foreign policy, whether it is really for our defense or not. We no longer merely defend ourselves—we defend our "interests" as well, whenever the administration in power deems it appropriate. It is time for us to return to a more limited interpretation of defense so that we can begin to reduce our arms industries and stop fueling foreign wars with our weapons.

We have to tell our representatives that we want to export useful technologies, medicines and education in place of warplanes, tanks and missiles. With this change in attitude we would be walking the way we are talking. If we can do this, we can once again be credible when we speak of promoting love, peace, unity, understanding and hope for the people of the world.

TRADE

At the present time we find that we are at a competitive disadvantage with Japan, and we are getting increasingly concerned about this in the midst of our current recession. We find we are dealing with very tough competitors from the point of view of quality, negotiation skills and the desire to look out for oneself. The Japanese are teaching us many worthwhile lessons. It's interesting that while we allow the Japanese to export many of their cars with our reasonable rules and restrictions, they do not allow the importation of American vehicles by standards anywhere close to ours. Fair trade should mean fair trade. We should be allowed to export our products and services to Japan on exactly the same basis that they are allowed to export their cars to the United States. Let's clear the playing field for negotiation and stop playing by rules and standards that were set up many years ago, and which are no longer valid in the current market situation.

Trade rules are not the only thing that contribute to the economic imbalance between our two countries. The difference in savings habits between Americans and Japanese magnifies the problem. Japan's average worker saves approximately 17% of his annual income; an average American worker saves less than 3%. It's easy to see how, in a very short period of time, the Japanese can out-invest, out-buy and gradually take over the assets of our country if they so choose.

As a nation, we need to form a consensus to act; we need to change our laws to give incentives for savings instead of being heavily taxed for it.   If we do this, and develop fair trade rules, we can compete with anyone in the world.

For the past several years we have spoken of "trade wars" as though trade with other countries is innately warlike.   Trade is supposed to be for the benefit of both trading parties.   The very word, trade, means that each party gives something of value and gets something of value in exchange.   In the modern world, the game is not so much trading things of equal value as it is for each country to try to maximize exports and minimize imports. This is a win-lose strategy.   The irony is that countries pursuing this strategy will find that the more successful they are in obtaining a high export/import ratio, the more they will be ruining the economies of the countries to which they export. As the economies of other countries deteriorate, they will no longer be able to buy imports. Thus the hard-driving, exporting country is killing the goose that lays the golden eggs.

At some point, every nation in the world will be forced to realize that the only long term trading policy is an equitable one that results in win-win. Even as we adopt certain restrictions to "level the trading playing field," we need to keep focused on modifying our system of international trade so that everyone wins.

INTERNATIONAL RELATIONS

When a government steamrolls over the rights of its own citizens and/or those of neighboring countries, it creates fear and weakness, and eventually, terrorism. Yet we as a nation have supported both leftist and rightist foreign governments even when they are despotic and cruel. We seem to others to have become an opportunistic nation and have lost the special moral and ethical qualities that once set us above the typical, selfish political strife that goes on between nations.

Our relations with other countries seem now to be based almost exclusively on our economic interests, our ideological preferences and our parochial and naive views of how others should live. A case in point is our policy aimed at eradicating the drug industry in Peru and Columbia. In September 1991, we visited Peru, which was in the midst of an undeclared war and was being massively disrupted by terrorists and the government fighting each other. It has been a long war in which both sides are slowly destroying each other, building hatred and pursuing goals that are unachievable with their present approach.

We saw impoverished people in the countryside doing what they can to provide for their families by growing the most valuable crop they know—cocoa leaves—which are later processed into cocaine. "The Shining Path," the terrorist group, is encouraging and helping these people to grow cocoa so that they can feed their families and not continue the starvation and poverty that is common among them (also, the Shining Path reaps a huge profit from cocaine trafficking). From the point of view of the farmers, growing cocoa leaves is the most reasonable thing to do to support their families and reduce their poverty. They are far removed from and don't even think about the consequences that are happening in this country or other places in the world from cocaine. The farmers who grow cocoa leaves won't stop because of governmental harassment, but only when they see a worthwhile alternative.

In Lima, Peru we couldn't go into a Kentucky Fried Chicken without there being one or two armed guards present. Other stores had several armed guards and the banks had a whole company. The whole country is armed with groups fighting each other. This is a futile, non-winnable war with the approach we are taking, both because of the problems causing the unrest and the cocaine crop problem. We have spent millions beefing up the weaponry and training the national police and the army but it is like throwing money down the drain. When we were in Peru we witnessed the poverty, the fear, and people everywhere carrying guns. So fewer people are able to do productive work and more people are involved with defending themselves, their businesses and the undeclared war. The economy has badly deteriorated and everyone in the country is a loser.

Once again, we are involved in a non-workable for-

eign policy strategy. For all the money we have thrown at
this problem, we have succeeded only in temporarily
reducing a small percentage of the total amount of cocaine
entering the United States. We have been doing this for
years and even though we have seen, over and over, that
it doesn't work, our government is still following the
policy of enforced eradication of cocoa fields.

To begin to get our power back in our domestic drug
crisis and in our foreign policy, we need to help both sides
of a conflict to arrive at a win-win solution. In the case of
Peru, there are other crops that can be grown for good
profits if assistance is given to the rural population. We
also need to keep ideology in perspective and provide
practical assistance. We could spend our millions of dollars introducing new crops, building new wells, showing
the people how to market their produce directly instead of
giving away their profits to layers of middlemen. We
would be much farther along in eliminating cocaine production if we had used our money to build schools and
health clinics and grain storage silos. We need to speak
out, to use our power to let our representatives know that
we want to stop throwing money at old, unworkable
solutions. We need to encourage our representatives to
use their brightest and best people to figure out new win-
win solutions to problems in international relations.

Many helpful institutions already exist to foster good
relations between countries. The Peace Corps is one of
them; so are the Olympics. The cultural exchanges of
musicians, artists, teachers and students are helping to
break down the barriers between nations.

In general, however, we in the United States have been slow to recognize that we have as much to learn from other cultures as they have from us. Perhaps because we have heard our politicians praise our way of life as "the greatest in the world" for so long now, we have closed our minds to allow the light of other cultures to shine in. So a part of our enlightened foreign policy must be for each of us to realize that every culture in the world has something wonderful to contribute.

In summary,

*Having a foreign policy
which reflects our noblest goals
would further understanding,
cooperation and prosperity
for all people and all countries,
not just our own.*

We can, as a nation, begin to set a standard in the world by acting with integrity, being truthful and honest, and being a reliable friend to people around the world. As we said before, let's "walk the way we talk."

THE ENVIRONMENT AND OUR BOND WITH CREATION

Each year our planet becomes more polluted and in more danger of sustaining permanent damage to its life support system. At the same time, national and international organizations and governments are beginning to take countermeasures to at least slow down, if not reverse, the damage. Even with these efforts, however, because of rapidly expanding populations and industrialization of under-developed countries, and economic growth in developed countries, we are losing the battle. The follow chart shows the problem graphically.

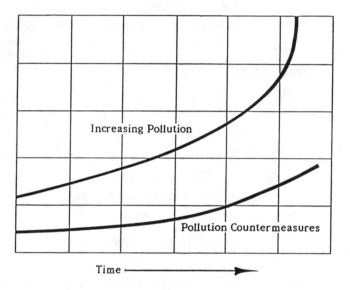

If we continue polluting at our present rates, the measures we take to reduce pollution will fall short of what is needed to stop its advance.

Are we seeing the big picture? Our planet has been brutally violated by her only predator, MAN. The destruction is continuing on many fronts: acid rain, toxic waste, industrial pollution, global warming, ozone depletion, rain forest destruction and extinction of species, to name just a few. In many ways, it's the holocaust of our planet. We have waged a one-sided war against our planet for too long.

*We must cease the wars and
win the battle
to preserve this planet—our giver of life.*

Recently we read about children becoming involved in environmental programs.[3] An eleven-year old girl in Baltimore wrote, "Why should I wait? I can see problems now and I want to help fix them. After all, it's my world too." There is a boy in Florida who single-handedly is helping to save the manatee, or sea cow, from extinction. Several fifth-graders in California have become WATT-BUSTERS, monitoring their school for persons (including teachers) who waste energy or use it inefficiently, and giving out tickets and awards each year. There is a group of inner-city kids in Philadelphia who recently reclaimed a local park from drug dealers and have cleaned it out, planted a garden and started a recycling program. A group of North Carolina students have started a tree planting program which they pass on to younger students when they graduate.

As these children grow and become the workers and leaders in the next half-century, they will infuse the country with a broadly-based spirit of environmentalism—of respect for the earth. Even with all of our pro-environment institutions, such as the Environmental Protection Agency, we haven't yet made enough of a serious national effort to halt pollution. We are still playing games with environmentalism, with some politicians using it as a tool for re-election.

Contrary to what many of our politicians would have

us believe, we do not have to lose jobs because of pro-environmental policies. In fact, many studies have been done which show that energy conservation and pollution control will be among the fastest growing industries throughout the world over the next decades.

It is time for each of us to use our power and assume responsibility for the health of our planet.

There is no greater task at hand
than our rush to save the earth.

Win-Win Solutions

We've spoken several times in this book about finding win-win solutions.

Don: Perhaps one reason I feel so strongly about this is because in the past I've been involved in so many lose-lose situations.

I have spent most of my adult years in the construction industry—as a subcontractor, a general contractor and now as a construction management consultant. In a typical new construction project, whether it be a residential home or a large commercial building, a client hires an architect to represent what he wants and thinks he can afford. There is sometimes a lack of clear understanding between the client and the architect because architects cannot always read their client's mind, and clients find it difficult to visualize the finished product from the plans or drawings.

Small details are not always shown, and it is almost impossible not to have some omissions, errors and, in particular, changes as the project unfolds. So the architect defends his work and wants more money for any additional work that is needed. The client, on the other hand, wants as much work as possible from the architect without paying more money. So the first adversarial relationship has a chance to develop.

The project is then awarded to a low bidder. For a contractor to be successful he has to do the work as reasonably as possible while making the customer happy. This maximizes his profit and his reputation for efficiency. It pays for him to cut corners, skimp wherever possible, and get the cheapest subcontractors. Some contractors produce substandard work if they can get away with it, and the cost savings that the contractor makes are sometimes not in the client's best interest. It also pays for the contractor to find problems with the plans and specifications, for this maximizes the amount he will be paid for changes or corrections. This causes an adversarial relationship to develop between the client and the contractor.

In my years of experience in construction, I witnessed almost every ploy that could be used to take advantage of the opposite party. This includes using liens unfairly, lack of payment, threats and even subtle blackmail in the course of a construction project. For example, the client may delay payments to the contractor and then offer immediate payment with a substantial discount, often an unreasonably large percentage. If the contractor is scrambling to pay his bills for materials and labor (as many are), he is forced to accept way less than he is entitled to so that he can get paid on time, meet his obligations and stay in business. It is a tough business, and the contractor knows that if he makes one serious mistake, he may be out of business altogether.

On the other side of the deal, the contractor may take advantage of every change, for which he charges extra, so that the client can no longer afford to complete the project. In this case, the contractor may actually make more profit if the project is canceled than if it had gone forward to completion. This has happened many times between the government and defense contractors.

Another part of this business is bidding for contracts. In some parts of the country subcontractors usually turn in their bids on a job to the general contractor a couple of weeks before the contract is to be awarded. If a particular subcontractor is close to the general contractor, he may be able to find out what each of his competitors' bids are. A half hour or so before the bid deadline and opening, that subcontractor phones in a change in his bid price both to have the lowest bid and to allow no time for any of the competitors to find out his latest bid price.

Even if the subcontractor does not get inside information and makes a high bid, he can claim that he has included extra items in his bid that are not included in the other bids, and thus beat out the lower bidder. If the subcontractor's bid is lower than anyone else's, he can say that he forgot to include several items and bring his total bid up to just under the next highest bid.

A general contractor wants to get the lowest cost possible. One way he can do this, if the bid openings are not public or supervised, is to claim that none of the bids are acceptable and then grind the bidders down to submit lower prices. If a general contractor knows the market he is dealing in, he can bid a job with no apparent profit and end up doing quite well.

I could cite many examples of government projects, originally coming in close to bid, eventually going over cost by 50% and more. This happens because government contract negotiators (and many others) may not be knowledgeable enough in this business. There are times when contracts are written so they will go over deliberately. Both sides know the costs are going over, yet this is all of the public funds that have been allocated for the project. Once it is underway they know they will have to come up with the money to complete the job. Some of these things happen behind closed doors, away from public scrutiny. No matter how many safeguards are in place or how many people are monitoring a project, there are still opportunities for dishonest conduct.

The construction industry isn't unique in this regard. American companies in many different industries work through Panamanian or Bahamian corporations because it makes their activities harder to track. Doing this gets around laws and allows companies to function as they feel they have to in order to compete in foreign countries and the real world. Many of these schemes are simply legal methods of getting around U.S. laws and government scrutiny.

In my own business, I have tried to turn the typical contract dealings around to produce win-win situations. For example, when, as a construction management consultant, I act as a client's representative, it gives the client construction expertise and someone looking out for their interests. We try to save money, save time and get the quality job he wants within his budget. At the same time, I insist that the contractors be paid on time and paid fairly for the work they perform. Because contractors who deal with me know this, and they have less risk, the padding that they build into their bids in case of delayed payment, delayed starting dates, etc., is not necessary. So I am able to get my clients lower bids and a better quality project than they would otherwise receive—it's a win-win scenario.

Retailers, wholesalers and manufacturers have found that when they stand behind their products or services and satisfy their customers, business flourishes. If one party is taking away from another, or from its customers, a loss is incurred, and both parties are looking out for their own interests at the expense of the other.

When people cooperate in integrity for their mutual benefit, a multiplying effect occurs, and everyone prospers.

There are more and more examples of win-win agreements occurring in our country today. Unions are working with companies for their mutual success. School systems and teachers are getting back on track with regard to their purpose. One of the biggest benefits for all of us is the pride and inner power that comes from people doing their best and being appreciated, being right with themselves and being part of the success they can bring about. In the long run, this takes far less effort than foot-dragging and fighting each other.

In chapter 6, we mentioned that as we begin to retrieve our personal power, it whispers to us that it must be used for the good of all, and that if we do not use it lovingly and generously, we will lose it. In this chapter we have tried to give examples of how empowered people can help to make a better world. There is a lot to be done—it is quite a challenge. Being in our power also tells us something more. We will have the determination, the energy and the confidence to take up the challenge.

We will be heard, and we will make a difference.

8

THE ROAD TO EMPOWERMENT

Growing Up

Empowerment for an individual is a continuing process not a fixed state at which we arrive. There are times we experience more power and times we experience less. Sometimes we give our power away. Sometimes we just let it slip away. No part of us is ever static—we are always shifting, changing. Just like an athlete, however, the more we train and the more we develop good habits, the more we will be empowered consistently and to higher levels.

The road to empowerment consists of learning many basics; then getting into the habit of living by them. From there we need to stretch to newer levels by using our intuition and listening to our inner voice. For many of us this road has been long, rocky and rough. At the same time there has been lots of fun and many worthwhile times in the process of getting to where we are now. There are still lots of opportunities to grow and look forward to experiencing more spiritual power. It's valuable for each of us to look at the path we've traveled to get to where we are now.

Chrystol: My path has taken me from total disempowerment in childhood to having self-love, self-esteem and knowing who I am today. It is, of course, no accident that I have co-authored this book, because self-empowerment has been such a struggle in my life. Though I still have to work at it, I now experience my power and spirituality on a regular basis. As Gloria Steinem said in her book, Revolution From Within, *we teach what we need to learn and write what we need to know. Writing this book has been one of the most empowering, inspiring and enriching experiences of my life.*

Don: My family was a good one. My parents were married for fifty years— ours was a healthy environment and there was no alcoholism or violence. Even within this environment, I developed filters which screened everything I saw and heard, and altered reality to suit my needs of the moment. A half-century later, I am still working at eliminating some of my filters.

Each step of the way in my life I have learned something. When I did well at something, it taught me a great deal about myself; when I faltered I probably learned more. The road to growth is slow, painful and frustrating, and at the same time, rewarding and exciting. When we reflect on our experiences, we may say "I was an alcoholic," "I lost my job," "I failed at this," "I've been divorced," "My kids have been through things because of the way I acted," or "I've hurt other people," In looking back, we will always see something that we could have done differently, some things we might have done better. Yet for some reason we have come through these experiences. In hindsight, I now see mine for what they really were—opportunities to learn, to check my perspective and to continually adjust my goals and orientation. They were also teaching me to be more careful about myself and others. All of my experiences, in the aggregate, I now see as having a single aim—helping me to grow up.

When life becomes a process, the old distinctions between winning and losing, success and failure, fade away. Everything, even a "negative" outcome, has the potential to teach us and to further our quest. [1]

In our society, as we age, we speak of "getting old." But more commonly, we speak of "growing old." The expression is so familiar we don't pay attention to the words themselves. But there is a big difference between getting old and growing old. The former implies it just happens inevitably, but growing old implies something we do, something in which we have an active part.

In America in former generations there was a great deal of respect for our elders. Even today in many other cultures the respect one is shown is in proportion to age—the older the person the more respect he or she receives. Perhaps this is so universal because at some level we know that "growing up" is truly "growing."

A friend and poet speaks of growing old in these terms:

I have a vision of the aged, for I see that they have discovered, in every event of every day, a new lesson of life to be welcomed and mastered.

I see the passage of time is not without its own reason, and I see the beauty of each soul beginning to be reflected in their wise and kindly faces.

I see their wisdom turned to the good of others so that they have no further need to dwell upon themselves.

And I see that, as the years pass by, they do not slow down but quicken to the promise of the next step of the never-ending road.

I imagine them moving into the Golden Years when all who look upon them may know that growing old is really growing.

I see their peace and their love as a beacon of inspiration to everyone they meet.

*And finally, I see that their presence is a signal that the last
years in this domain are the finest years, and that
when their stay on earth is finished, it is for them a
new beginning.* [2]

We are all getting older. We have no choice about that,
but we can place our emphasis on growing older with
grace.

LIVING IN THE MOMENT

Living for right now...it's so very simple, yet so very
difficult to do. Many of us have been taught, indirectly and
directly, to always plan for the future. A date book is one
device for not living in the moment. In addition to helping
us remember appointments, plan schedules, etc., they
actually enable us to defer our lives to the future. We spend
a good part of our time in the present planning for the
future.

We have the same problems with living in the past.
It's good to learn from the past and enjoy our good
memories. However, most of us spend too much time
analyzing our mistakes: "If I had only done this, or that...."

Doing either of these weakens our power both to
enjoy and to contend with any moment in which we find
ourselves. Being fully present is a critical key to empowerment. Whatever we give our attention to is that which
receives our energy.

We truly only have the present.

How often are we really in the present with all of our senses, thoughts and feelings focused on NOW? Actually, we are in the present all the time. We truly can live only in the moment. We feel, we sense, we experience, and all of our faculties exist in each present moment.

There really is no past or future—there is just a series of present-moments, all strung together, which include thoughts of the past and thoughts about the future. One of the best gifts we can give to anyone else we deal with is being entirely present with them, listening to them, experiencing them and knowing them in the moment. How many times are we with someone but not really with them? And how often have we complained that someone we are with is "out to lunch," "vacant," or "somewhere else?"

One of the skills we need to learn is how to really listen. Whether we listen to Christ, Buddha, Krishna, Moses, Mohammed or any great guru or teacher, they will usually touch on the importance of living in the moment, being present, and experiencing the here and now. This is an essential part of experiencing our power, feeling our inner guide, being in touch with God and being in touch with the beauty of nature and the love of friends and family.

How fully we enjoy life
is dependent on having
our body, mind and spirit
in the present.

Self-empowerment exists in each present moment. We are all capable of living more in the NOW. As mentioned above, it is something that is very simple and yet difficult to do. It takes practice. If we can't always be perfectly in the moment, there is something we can do. We can commit ourselves to practice.

MINISTERING TO OURSELVES

We are the centers of our own universe. It's not right or wrong—it just is. We can dislike ourselves and harm ourselves. Or we can give ourselves a little credit and help ourselves improve. The purpose of life is to learn and most of us learn by making mistakes. If we are attuned to what is happening, we can learn from our mistakes and make the necessary corrections. Most of us have lied and we have learned for the most part not to lie; it works better. We can improve all sorts of things about ourselves by paying attention to our inner prompting and to the input from others.

Each of us has the ability to judge ourselves fairly. We can look at ourselves and say we are too fat, too slow or too lazy. We can look at our opinions of ourselves and see which are valid or which are not valid. It isn't constructive to beat ourselves for failings; yet observing that we are fatter than we want to be, or less loving or less active than we want to be can be constructive. This enables us to make a change or see why we are tending to be the way we are. If we are not good in math, it may be an old block or tape that limits us but which can be erased. Most of the traits in our lives can be looked at to see which really serve us, what is basically true, and which things we believe about ourselves that are not really true.

From analysis and self-monitoring we can get to the point of self-help. There are also many different kinds of help available. Working with a therapist can be constructive if it doesn't become a dependence to keep from helping yourself. Joining groups can also help us; groups like 12-Step programs or even groups like Boy Scouts, bicycling clubs, golfing—all sorts of things can help us be better people. Attending school and classes can be of help.

In realizing the whole world is open to us, we can choose the things we want to do. We can listen to our inner guides and set worthwhile goals for ourselves. What type of activities really fit us? What really makes us feel worthwhile? What inspires us the most? It is a wonderful adventure to find out these things, and act on them.

An excellent book on approving of and healing ourselves is *You Can Heal Yourself* by Louise L. Hay. It shows how we can look in the mirror and see our good traits and love ourselves, and at the same time work on the way we are and heal the things that bother us about ourselves. We can do this alone, with groups or with professional help. Whichever way we choose, the opportunities are there.

THE RIGHT TIME

> *There's a time for some things*
> *and a time for all things;*
> *a time for great things,*
> *and a time for small things.*

Cervantes, in *Don Quixote*

Life is a process. We go through valleys, hills, canyons, beautiful areas and painful areas, all of them contributing to experience and growth.

Don: In my path, it has taken me 50+ years to get to the point where I can get back the power I gave to other people. I gave my power away to employers, to women, to other men, to anyone and everyone I thought deserved to control me more than I deserved to control myself.

Everything has its right time. If we could roll out the past and future like a rug onto the floor, we would be able to see our entire life span. If we could see this, we would also see the connections between events in our lives, and we would understand why some things happened early and why some have not yet come. We don't have the ability (at least not yet) to see all of our life's connections, but we do have some guidelines which help. One of these is to realize that everything that has ever happened to us is purposeful, and that its purpose will sooner or later become evident.

Another guideline is to know that if our needs are still unmet, then something needs to happen to clear the way for them to manifest.

*Our personal power is
a divine gift which is always there,
waiting patiently to manifest within us.*

We cannot foresee how and when it will come—whether gradually, by stages or in one grand sweep. But we can influence its coming, so that we will become empowered sooner rather than later. We do this by reaching inward for our highest selves and reaching outward to do our best in the world. Each reinforces the other.

The "right time" is coming for each of us. It is reaching out to us. We can help by reaching back and meeting it halfway. All things happen "In God's good time," and God's good time is when we are ready.

BLAMING OURSELVES

The world is difficult enough without our adding to our burden by blaming ourselves for our lives; blaming ourselves for sins, selfishness, inaction, incompetence and a host of other negatives. True, some of the things we may have been doing and are doing we don't judge to be right, but this doesn't make us an overall bad person, and no one of us is inherently bad. Many of the things we don't like about ourselves are changeable—with the right approach. Continuing to berate ourselves isn't the right approach. In fact, doing this is one of the most destructive acts in which we participate.

Every major religion tells us that we are children of God, that we each have a spark of divinity within us; that God, in the form of inner guidance, speaks to us. This gives each of us the opportunity to change ourselves, to rise to be our best selves. We don't have to be alone in this work. Groups and therapy can help us, plus we can develop techniques that can help us through this ourselves.

We have no reason to blame ourselves for anything. One of the wisest and truest statements to come down to us through the ages is: We are responsible for doing the best we can—we are not responsible for the results. If we are not doing the best we can, we can begin now.

Playing Our Old Tapes

We have all been programmed from our past. Some of these programs are helpful and some are harmful. If we take constructive time to look carefully at our past limitations, we can free ourselves from these. Which of these labels belong to our parents, friends, employers or others? We can be stuck in our lives by many of these labels which we have put on ourselves or have allowed to be put on us during the course of our lives.

This book is a result of us looking at the limits in our own lives, the restrictions, and the disempowering things that we allowed to happen to us. By quitting our old, dissatisfying routines and making fundamental changes in our lives, we are now headed in a completely different direction. It has been scary.

Limits are boxes in which we put ourselves. Sometimes we can only give up one box, or just a few boxes, at a time. Sometimes we have to stick to things with which we're familiar. And sometimes we allow ourselves to remain in bad situations.

Listening inside to what is right for us makes us feel good, brings us joy and helps identify our aspirations in life. This helps us to see that many of the restrictions we have put on ourselves are no longer needed. We can change jobs, where we live, and sometimes, when necessary, families, but most importantly, we can change ourselves.

When we listen carefully to our inner voice, we know which old tapes should be thrown out. We may think we still need them and that it is wrong to get rid of them. Again, one of the things self-empowerment brings us is the courage to dump our old tapes and have the confidence to (as Joseph Campbell put it) "Follow our bliss."

No old tape, no box or other limitation
is worthy of keeping,
unless it adds to our present fulfillment.

OVERCOMING LOSSES AND SETBACKS

Most of us have found that losing loved ones emotionally while they are still physically present (such as escaping through drugs or caused by a mental illness) is one of the greatest tragedies of life. "Why me, God?" is one of the questions we ask ourselves when we suffer a tragic loss. And, receiving no apparent answer, we tend to close ourselves emotionally in order to stifle our pain.

Why have we been given the capacity to feel such grief? Perhaps because grief is a tool for growth. Many times, in the midst of grief, the experience seemed impossible and caused so much pain that we couldn't bear it. In retrospect, we realize that we learned valuable lessons from it which enabled us to be ready for the next experience in life, the next encounter, the next relationship and the next level of personal growth.

Facing grief head-on is a healthy process in spite of the pain we feel. We cannot eliminate our emotions but we can acknowledge them and allow ourselves to experience them. When we do this, a strange thing happens—they lose some of their power over us. The more we are able to openly and directly face our strong feelings, the less terrible they feel. It is our straining against them that feeds and prolongs pain.

When we learn to feel our emotions fully, we discover that they have a great capacity for guiding and teaching us. As we learn to release old patterns, our feelings become invaluable for telling us where we are, in any given moment.

Setbacks and problems are inevitable and part of the challenges of life. Rather than being negative, many of them are an indication we should look at our premises or what we are doing. What are we doing? Is it right? Why is it a loss or challenge? Have we not paid attention? Is someone crying for help or attention? The things we can learn and the growing we can do is the gift from difficulties and challenges. They can truly be a blessing if we respond positively to the signals. They can lead us to the action to save a marriage, a business or a pending disaster for our kids.

We either get the best of our problems or they get the best of us.

Changing Times

Until recently, the old standards such as "You must work forty hours a week or you are lazy," "Consistency is better than creativity," "You're just a dreamer—get practical," and "Stop rebelling and respect tradition" were considered mandatory rules for success. Facts and figures have been king, and anyone who placed any value on intuition, mysticism, paranormal phenomena, psychic research, nontraditional spirituality or nonlinear thinking of any kind was labeled a kook, a loony, a crackpot and, sometimes, accused of being in league with the devil.

The doctrine of man's "dominion"
over the earth
has begun to change to man's
"stewardship" of the earth.
It is no longer ours to pillage
but to preserve. [3]

A great deal of intolerance and narrow-mindedness still exists but slowly, things are getting better. Today, scientists speculate about unknown energy fields and debate the nature of reality, almost as monks did in medieval times. Holistic concepts, long derided or ignored, are being used to create the products of the future. This opens tremendous opportunities and challenges for people of all ages.

We can make great strides forward
as a nation
if we are willing to find our power
and use it for the good of all.

Achieving Wholeness

We all need to borrow a page from the ancient Greeks, who believed that health and success were not possible unless attention was given to the whole person. When the individual was centered and balanced, then mind, body and spirit would remain healthy. Being centered, being right with our inner guides and recognizing ourselves as spiritual beings bring that wholeness to us. It activates our personal power.

Personal power is what makes great athletes, creative geniuses and inspiring leaders. Personal power does not mean strength in the limited, physical sense. It means the kind of strength we have when we know, with absolute certainty, who we are, that our capabilities are unlimited, and that we are each a precious and needed part of God's Creation.

Life is a symphony
where each molecule has its own
melody.
If we but listen
we will hear the harmony of it all. [4]

Self-Empowerment Is Empowerment of Others

Many of us are frequently discouraged because the problems around us seem so vast and intractable. Since most of us don't hold influential positions, how can we make a difference in the world? How can our single voice be heard amidst the din of indifference? Sometimes our contributions are obvious, as when someone opens a soup kitchen for the hungry, or when individuals form a group to curtail drug use in the neighborhood. Sometimes they are not at all obvious, even to the extent of never becoming known, as in this story:

A small town—Jasper—was experiencing a wave of community depression. It was not something that had happened all of a sudden. No, it had crept up on the townsfolk day by day, month after month and year after year. It had started when the town's single factory had closed down, and it had gained momentum when the drought hit three years in a row.

Folks just seemed to give up all hope, remaining in their houses most of the time and existing on subsistence incomes. A happy face was rarely seen, and this state of affairs had been going on for several years when the woman came to town.

No one knew for sure why she had come. Her name was Meg and she had just arrived one day and rented a small cottage in back of the Quigley's barn. Meg was middle-aged, middle-sized and of moderate attractiveness—she was hard to describe because she looked so, well, so average. She seemed to have no obvious means of support, and each day she walked through the village, smiling and offering a shy, whispered "hello" to everyone she passed by.

Meg stayed pretty much to herself and didn't return the occasionally flirtatious looks of the mayor or of Pete, the owner of the single auto repair shop. Nor did she join the Thursday night ladies' bingo game. And so, after awhile, everyone stopped paying much attention to her. But within a month of her arrival, things seemed to be going better in Jasper than they had been.

There was a quickness in the air, and the townsfolk seemed more invigorated than usual. When the men went to Paul's barbershop for a haircut, they didn't linger but went on their way with comments like, "I got to get back to painting the store," or "Sorry, Paul, I don't have time today—I'm fixing my pickup."

Gradually, without any outside investment, the town of Jasper was picking itself up by its own bootstraps. Jennie started shipping her terrific rhubarb pies to the city, thirty miles east, and Phil Marnie sold the software package he had been working on to a major corporation in far-off Seattle—not only that, but he hired three people to help him.

Jasper, became a happy, prosperous place. The original building facades on the main street were rebuilt, and for the first time in anyone's memory, tourists actually stopped for a cool drink or a sandwich instead of driving through the town to their next destination. When they did stop, these visitors remarked on how refreshed and comfortable they felt in the town. It was as though Jasper had discovered a marvelous elixir and had added it to the air.

Now all during this time, Meg never revealed why she had come to Jasper. While she stayed there she never once advised her neighbors or commented on the state of the town. And not a single person (not even Meg herself) understood that she was the source of the town's new well-being and prosperity.

Many years ago she had asked God for the opportunity to be of service to the world. But as far as she knew, that opportunity had never come. Yet this woman understood, at a deep level, that all the residents of her adopted town were no more than parts of herself, and that she was no more or less than a part of God.

And because Meg lived and breathed her understanding of oneness, she, by her mere presence, had a profound influence upon the town of Jasper. In fact, her influence was so great that several among the townsfolk attained their own state of understanding. Some of them moved to other towns, of course, and so the radiance and vitality and prosperity of Jasper was spread and multiplied. [5]

Gradually, ever so gradually, the influence of spiritual empowerment is making itself felt. Even now, there are many like Meg, living quietly and inconspicuously in their communities, raising the level of life by the simple agency of their presence.

Our subtle radiance has its effects.

A REMINDER OF SELF-EMPOWERING ACTIONS

Get active. Whenever you read or hear of some injustice or some law you want changed, let your representatives know about it. Here's one way to do it. Keep a stack of pre-stamped postal cards in a convenient place (like on the TV for when you see something you want to respond to). Next to the postal cards, keep a list of federal, state and local representatives' names and addresses. Your library can supply these to you. When politicians weigh the views of their constituents, postal cards received on an issue count as much as long letters. Another way is to phone your representative. It costs little, and someone will take the message. Also talk about it to your friends or anyone interested. When you have energy on a subject, do something constructive about it.

Remember all the good things you have done and realize the good things that you can still do.

Acknowledge that you have a power, a spiritual power within you, that automatically guides you in the direction of your own best interests.

Let your mind open up to non-structured thoughts where feelings, appreciation, love, joy and happiness can come in. This can be an openness, an appreciation of nature and beauty around you, prayer, meditation or even daydreaming. Some say praying is asking and meditating is listening.

Be consistent with your thoughts and actions. If it doesn't feel right to you, you probably shouldn't do it. Think it through, process it and be right with yourself.

Do things you feel good about. Smile at people. Notice and enjoy the things around you.

Be good to yourself and do good things for others without sacrificing yourself.

Where conflicts occur, look for win-win solutions.

Acknowledge your good traits and your spirituality on a daily basis. Practice constant appreciation of life.

Be with people who increase your energy and confidence and optimism. Stay away from those who drain you or make you feel angry, afraid or doubtful.

Life is a constant cycle of renewal at the same time we shed off the old. We can renew ourselves, our communities, our institutions and our earth. We have the opportunity for many beginnings. Little steps move us forward. Small steps by many combine to make great energy and progress. Each of us create the tiles in the mosaic of life. Together, we will create great things.

We hope you will look at different, better ways of doing things, that you will take the risk and try different approaches. Don't shy away from the new in order to protect the old—they both have their value and their place in our lives. True power doesn't start with government or wealth or influence or fame—it starts within each of us. Let's be true to ourselves, and not allow others to take away our power.

As we have said earlier, this is your life—it isn't a dress rehearsal—this is it! Take advantage of it by enjoying yourself and having fun with life—don't let it slip away while you are mired in the past or the future.

Look for the good and the beautiful in everything you see and everyone you meet. Let your love flow to its absolute maximum. Feel the life force of the earth and everything on it. Honor the Creation, honor yourself as part of it, and dream your dreams.

I know of no other way
to approach great tasks
than as play.
—Albert Einstein

One Final Question and an Implied Answer

Do you doubt that if we all got together and used our combined intelligence, creativity and energy to solve the problems of the world that we could not do it?

Authors' Note and Invitation

Only a few examples and ideas are presented in this book. All of us read or hear many stories of heroism, solutions to challenges and successful experiences, daily. Let's encourage our media to present more of these.

If you would like to share some of what you read or hear, as well as your own experiences, comments and suggestions with us, we will welcome and appreciate them. Hearing how others are solving their problems and becoming empowered can serve as examples to all of us. Our dream is to discuss and share self-empowerment, and win-win solutions with more and more people until all of our joint successes multiply for all our benefit. We hope to meet each of you someday.

APPENDIX

CHAPTER NOTES

Chapter 4

1. John Powell, S.J., *Why Am I Afraid to Tell You Who I Am*, Argus Communications, Allen, Texas, 1969.

2. M. Scott Peck, M. D., *The Road Less Traveled*, Simon & Schuster, New York, 1978.

Chapter 5

1. Dove Grace, *Pearls of Peace*, Carmel Valley, CA., 1990.

2. Marilyn Ferguson, *The Aquarian Conspiracy*, J. P. Tarcher, Inc. Los Angeles, CA, 1980.

3. Kahlil Gibran, *The Wisdom of Gibran*, Bantam Books, New York, 1973.

4. Dr. Wayne W. Dyer, *You'll See It When You Believe It*, Avon Books, New York, 1989.

Chapter 6

1. Dove Grace, *Pearls of Peace*, Carmel Valley, CA, 1990.

2. Roy Williams, *Preparing Your Family to Manage Wealth*, Monterey Pacific Institute, Marina , CA, 1992.

Chapter 7

1. Roy Williams, *Preparing Your Family to Manage Wealth*, Monterey Pacific Institute, Marina , CA, 1992, p. 167.

2. *Wall Street Journal*, Monday, May 4, 1992.

3. John Javna, syndicated newspaper column, *Earthworks*.

Chapter 8

1. Marilyn Ferguson, *The Aquarian Conspiracy*, J. P. Tarcher, Los Angeles, CA, 1980.

2. Colin Ingram, *Fables for the New Age*, Monterey Pacific Institute, Marina, CA, 1992.

3. Robert Browning, *Herakles*, 1871.

4. Dove Grace, *Pearls of Love*, Carmel Valley, CA, 1990.

5. Colin Ingram, *Fables for the New Age*, Monterey Pacific Institute, Marina, CA, 1992.

Suggested Reading

A Course in Miracles, Foundation for Inner Peace

The Aquarian Conspiracy, Marilyn Ferguson

Awaken the Giant Within, Anthony Robbins

The Different Drum, M. Scott Peck, M.D.

Earth in the Balance, Al Gore

Emmanuel's Book, compiled by Pat Rodegast and Judith Stanton

Illusions, Richard Bach

Living, Loving & Learning, Leo Buscaglia, Ph.D.

Love is Letting Go of Fear, Gerald G. Jampolsky, M.D.

The Prophet, Kahlil Gibran

Return to Love, Marianne Williamson

Revolution From Within, Gloria Steinem

The Road Less Travelled, M. Scott Peck, M.D.

Spiritual Growth, Sanaya Roman

What You Say About Me Is None Of My Business, Terry Cole-Whittaker

Why Am I Afraid To Tell You Who I Am, John Powell

Your Erroneous Zones, Dr. Wayne W. Dyer

ABOUT THE AUTHORS

Chrystol and Don Harris

Chrystol Clark Harris

A social activist since the age of 18, Chrystol has devoted much of her energy to volunteer concerns throughout the years. Early on, she spent three years involved with the Selkirk Mental Hospital in Manitoba, Canada, while simultaneously pursuing a full-time career. Later, in Calgary, she did volunteer rehabilitation work in a women's correctional facility, and has regularly served on non-profit boards in Canada and the United States.

Careerwise, for the past 25 years, Chrystol has worked internationally in management, and administration in the human resource development field. Since 1986 she has been managing her own personnel agency in Carmel, California. Throughout her career, she has given seminars, lectures, and appeared on television and radio talk shows in both the U.S. and Canada.

Born and raised in Winnipeg, Manitoba, Chrystol came to live in the U.S. in 1983, after having spent several years in Vancouver, Montreal and Calgary respectively.

Currently residing in Carmel, California with her husband, Don and son, Trevor, she enjoys expressing herself through poetry and oil painting.

Don R. Harris

Don is actively interested in human potential and social improvement. He has spent considerable time involved with youth groups and programs to help people realize their potential. This has included Boy Scouts, along with international groups concerned with improving the world environment.

His career in business and construction has spanned 28 years, taking him throughout the U.S. and the Middle East. He has functioned as a manager and officer for national and international companies, as well as owned a commercial construction company which was licensed and working in five states.

Currently, he is a management consultant principally for the construction industry. A seasoned speaker, he has appeared on television talk shows, given seminars and lectured extensively in the U.S. and internationally.

Raised in Seattle, Washington and Sourthern California, he received a degree in International Trade and Business Administration.

Between them, Chrystol and Don have travelled around the world, visiting 57 countries. The emphasis in their travels has been on learning social customs and culture, participating in local programs and listening to the concerns and problems of people. They now focus their time on giving talks, consulting, presenting seminars and helping individuals and groups achieve empowerment.

Consulting and Seminars

Self-Empowerment and Organization-Empowerment are among the most worthwhile, least developed principles in successful business and organizations today. This along with a win-win approach to problem solving and relationships can enhance job satisfaction and accomplishment. When the positive effort of all involved enhance and build on each other, results can be phenomenal. Goals, quality and creativity change remarkably when adversarial interaction is replaced by cooperation, trust and team work.

These principles will not eliminate conflict, on the contrary, they promote healthy conflict by bringing to the surface hidden agendas, unstated rules and suppressed inconsistencies that distract from productivity and creativity. People all know these problems exist and to some extent they always will (we're all human) but we can understand them and work with them while being true to our human feelings.

Addressing these concepts and issues through consulting and seminars can create new vitality, understanding and results, both individually and in your organization. Conflict resolution takes on new meaning through understanding trust-building and win-win solutions. Down to earth, realistic, practical solutions are more realizable than ever when all of our mental abilities are used instead of just our linear, logical knowledge.

We will work with you, your needs and your goals through private or small group meetings and seminars. Contact us for for discussions and information how we might work with you and your organization.

Harris Consultants & Seminars
225 Crossroads Blvd., # 136   Carmel, CA 93923
(408) 626-6738

DAILY EMPOWERMENT REMINDERS

1. Remember to honor myself as a spiritual being.
2. Take responsibility for my Life.
3. Listen for and follow the direction of my inner guide.
4. Be open to learning and to new experiences.
5. Have passion about myself, my experience and my life.
6. Seek a win-win outcome in all situations.
7. Appreciate the experiences in my life and Creation around me.
8. Seek integrity and balance in all my affairs.
9. Include meditation, prayer, visualization and affirmation in my daily routine.
10. Have fun—live in the moment—enjoy today.
11. Forgive myself for falling short in any of the above.
12. Remember to honor Love today.

TODAY—Do One Thing to Improve Your Life

Do One Thing to Improve Your World—IT'S EMPOWERING!

SELF - EMPOWERMENT

Reclaim Your Personal Power

Revitalize Your Community, Your Country and the World

by Chrystol Clark Harris and Don R. Harris

Copyright © 1993

Carmel Highlands Publishing

P. O. Box 22664, Carmel, Ca., 93923

(408) 626-6738

ORDER FORM

To Order

SELF-EMPOWERMENT

> *Reclaim Your Personal Power*
> *Revitalize Your Community, Country & the World*

$ 10.95 U. S. $13.95 Canada
California Residents add 7.75 %
Add $ 2.50 for shipping & Handling
(3 or more books, we pay the shipping)

Number of Copies Ordered_____

Amount Enclosed_____

Please send *Self-Empowerment* to:

Name:_____

Address:_____

City, State, Zip:_____

Make check payable & mail to:

Carmel Highlands Publishing

P. O. Box 22664, Carmel, California 93922

Thank You.